PENGUIN BOOKS

How To...
Calm It

T0017831

HOW TO... CALM IT

RELAX YOUR MIND

GRACE VICTORY

PENGUIN BOOKS

UK | USA | Canada | Ireland | Australia
India | New Zealand | South Africa

Penguin Books is part of the Penguin Random House group of companies
whose addresses can be found at global.penguinrandomhouse.com

First published in the UK by #Merky Books in 2021
Published in Penguin Books 2022
003

Text design © Andreas Brooks

Typeset in 10/13 pt Source Serif Variable Roman by Jouve (UK), Milton Keynes
Printed and bound in Great Britain by Clays Ltd, Elcograf S.p.A.

The authorised representative in the EEA is Penguin Random House Ireland,
Morrison Chambers, 32 Nassau Street, Dublin D02 YH68

A CIP catalogue record for this book is available from the British Library

ISBN: 978–1–529–90748–3

www.greenpenguin.co.uk

This book is dedicated to **YOU.** May you have the courage to be the creator of your own life and the belief that you are capable of doing so.

CONTENTS

FOREWORD BY BLACK MINDS MATTER UK   IX

INTRODUCTION   I

1   GETTING TO KNOW YOU   13
2   EVERYTHING IS CONNECTED   39
3   DETANGLING YOUR HEAD   75
4   CREATING BOUNDARIES   105
5   LETTING GO   119
6   DEALING WITH TRAUMA   133
7   YOU HAVE IT IN YOU TO HEAL   143

CONCLUSION   152

EVERYDAY RESOURCES   154

ACKNOWLEDGEMENTS   157

NOTES   160

FOREWORD

When we set out to raise funds for therapy sessions for Black people, by Black therapists, we weren't quite sure how it would be received, and whether we were the ones to do it.

We started Black Minds Matter UK in June 2020 during the height of two global pandemics – a virus sweeping the world, and the enduring torment of racial injustice in America that had tragically resulted in the senseless killings of George Floyd and Breonna Taylor. We were just two young women living in Bristol, feeling hurt, betrayal, confusion and loss about what was going on around us, and unable to attend protests to give voice to our anger and frustration.

With the Black Lives Matter movement on the world stage, our collective racial trauma was exacerbated. There were so many conversations happening about race, in so many spaces, both physical and digital. It was important to us that Black people's mental health was a major part of the discussions during this time, first and foremost so that we had space away from it all and an opportunity to heal, but also so that we had a chance to speak about other issues that may affect our lives – not just racial trauma – as it's vital to view Black people as multi-faceted human beings and not just victims of racial violence. We felt that the most valuable conversation would be between two Black people, and that there should be a safe space for someone to talk with a trained and certified therapist who not only looks like them, but could be nuanced in their approach and unpack their struggles, guiding them towards a better place of mental healing after years of neglect, abuse and suffering.

Our journey started as a simple text between friends: 'How amazing would it be if someone raised money for Black people to seek therapy and receive the healing they deserve?' We both had a deep passion for mental-health issues, having experienced them in our own lives. We turned to the tools we had at hand – our laptops, the internet, and our past fundraising experience – and got to it. We created a very basic website, a GoFundMe page, and an Instagram account, and then spread the word to our immediate family and friends. Our mission was clear from the get-go: to connect Black people with certified Black therapists, to encourage Black people to seek out medical treatment during the early stages of a mental illness, and to tackle the stigma surrounding mental health in and outside of the Black community. We couldn't have predicted the overwhelming response. Within forty-eight hours we had reached our initial fundraising goal, and our target to pair fifty people with Black therapists; however, we were inundated with requests for more support. It was astonishing to see our community galvanise behind our mission, and in less than six months we've grown our incredible team of volunteers and raised an astonishing £800k which will go towards changing over 2,000 lives within the UK.

When it comes to understanding and advocating for Black mental-health issues, there is still so much work and learning to be done. Firstly, everyone must acknowledge that it is a critical issue at a cultural level. For years, Black people have been viewed as strong and resilient beings, negating the necessity of thinking about our mental-health needs, and as a community we gloss over this. Secondly, we suffer from a proven form of race-based stress called racial trauma, which is the consequence of living in a society full of micro and macro racial aggressions. Thirdly, we have to acknowledge how much systemic racism has poured into our healthcare system. In the UK, Black British people are three to four times more likely to be diagnosed with psychosis, are detained under the mental health act more frequently than white people, and are often treated harshly and unsympathetically when they receive professional care[*]. Because of the lack of therapists of colour in the healthcare service, Black people often work one-on-one with therapists who don't share their lived experience – creating a disconnect in culture and nuance. It's a large task that will take time, but there is a solution, and it can be done.

[*]   https://youngminds.org.uk/blog/Black-mental-health-matters/

As Black Minds Matter UK continues to grow, we will encourage wider conversations that shift the perception of Black people in society, because you can't care about Black lives if you don't care about Black minds. If there's one thing we've learned this year, it is to never underestimate your power and your ability to make long-term change in society. We plan to continue providing more access for Black people in the UK to become certified Black therapists for as long as our service is needed. Our desire to see better representation in counselling and to combat the barriers to Black people entering the industry has led us to partner with Black Therapy Matters, to ensure that aspiring Black therapists are supported both emotionally and financially until they qualify. With increased access to certified Black therapists and growing funds in the form of donations, Black Minds Matter UK can continue to increase the number of people who will be able to access our service after our second launch in June 2021. With the right mission, resources and community, we plan to positively transform the face of Black mental health in the UK and beyond.

Black Minds Matter UK

INTRODUCTION

Firstly, hello and welcome. If you've reached this page it means you're intrigued about what I have to say and are interested in starting the wonderful journey of exploring yourself in a multi-dimensional way that will result in a calmer and more stable mind and body. That is not an easy thing to admit, or try to do, so thank you for putting yourself first. It's wonderful to have you with me.

Wellness is a complex and very personal topic, and one that's always changing. But, above all, it's an individual process. I want you to feel this book is for you, and I also want to encourage you to seek professional advice, either while or after reading (if you are in the position to do so). As I get older and practise my self-care routine rigorously, I am more in tune with my mind and my body and its shifts – dialling up or dialling down what I need to focus on most. And doing the work with someone qualified will ensure that you get the results you need.

WHO AM I?

Being a working-class, plus-size Black woman, I have often felt left out of wellness spaces and conversations because I do not fit a specific mould or ideal. So over the last few years I set about going public on my mental health, documenting my journey and then training as a therapist. My journey started after I hit rock-bottom in 2015. I was unhappy, but couldn't pinpoint *why*. It was that simple question of 'Why, Grace?' that took me on a journey, not only of self-discovery, but of enlightenment too. With the help of qualified therapists, spiritual healers, numerous books, online resources and my own intuition and self-awareness, I began to make sense of my feelings and to calm my mind – and my life – through self-care, therapy, holistic techniques and practices.

WESTERN WELLNESS

The wellness space has an image problem, often caused by photographs of its ideal: thin, white, slender women who are spread across Instagram or wellness platforms, chanting 'om'. Wellness has often excluded Black and brown bodies. And when we understand that wellness is often taught and practised from a Western stance, it creates a cultural gap where the dominant viewpoint ignores the varied nuances and many different sets of cultural approaches to healing. The wellness that I advocate takes into consideration so many strands – from indigenous practices, to established holistic techniques and one-on-one therapy. It's important to acknowledge that the way of making sense of our minds has been controlled by a dominant group, which has excluded the varying shades of others.

'WHOLE-ISTIC' WELLNESS

I define my approach to wellness and mindfulness as 'WHOLE-istic'. It's no surprise that this is closely related to the word *holistic*, which means dealing with and treating something in its entirety – not just a small part. To be WHOLE-istic considers the *whole* person and not merely one symptom or individual need. To be WHOLE-istic is to provide support to yourself, but to others too. To be WHOLE-istic takes into consideration our many nuances and cultural upbringing. Understanding wellness in this way expands it from focusing merely on the physical parts of a person, to including the emotional, spiritual and behavioural aspects too, and comprehending how they all combine to work together, and why we must make space and time to care for them all. Our bodies – in all their many shapes, sizes, genders and abilities – are marvellous things and are hugely interconnected. From our DNA, to our memories and our core beliefs: everything comes together to influence our relationship and approach to wellness.

I am incredibly passionate about this type of wellness because I believe it is for everyone – all you need are the tools and guidance to help you practise it yourself. Navigating life with more awareness of your mental and physical needs, and actively choosing a holistic approach as you decide to care for yourself, is a radical act. To live holistically is to value yourself enough to take care consistently of every part that makes you *you*. It does not mean putting a sticking plaster over a weeping wound, in the hope it will get better. Instead it means cleaning the wound, getting advice about it, nursing it and only then putting on the plaster. Living holistically does not mean clicking your fingers and clearing your mind instantly; it means taking time, being patient with yourself and doing the work to bring *you* back to you.

WHAT THIS BOOK ISN'T

It's important to state that this book isn't the be-all and end-all for your entire self-care, well-being and mindfulness needs. It isn't going to magically transform your life or give you all the answers for why you feel stressed, sad or sick. It is not packed full of beautiful anecdotes. It is not advocating a one-dimensional, one-size-fits-all cure for your mind. It's not endorsing the typical vision of wellness aimed at Western profit. It's not going to skip or make light of the African, Indian and indigenous teachings rooted in the practices and rituals that are now taught in the Western world. You won't always find kindness throughout these pages, because sometimes (and pay attention to the *sometimes*) brutal honesty is what we need. This book isn't going to suddenly fix your trauma, either, because that shit takes more than words on a page. This book isn't over-complicated by inaccessible language, which more often than not is used to create divides within spaces that are meant for us all.

WHAT THIS BOOK IS

This book is an insight and guide into how we can learn to calm our minds and choose to care for ourselves. It is full of tangible tools, tailored tips and intriguing information that breaks down well-being through a multi-dimensional lens, and which you can then practise whenever it suits you. This book is here to help break down and identify the possible reasons why so many of us are feeling disconnected, dissatisfied with aspects of life or distressed. This book is for the spiritually hungry, and for those looking for something deeper in order to understand the world. This book is here to help you detangle your head sufficiently to understand your feelings and set you on the path to professional help. Quite frankly, this is the book I needed five years ago, when I knew that I needed help in calming my mind, changing my thought patterns and putting myself first. I spent most of that time typing into Google, 'How do I meditate?', 'How do I align my chakras?' and following an internet rabbit warren of self-care. I thought these questions were the keys to a better me, but they didn't take into account a person like me at all. This book, however, puts you at the core.

WHAT I HOPE YOU GAIN FROM READING THIS

Ultimately I hope you gain a greater sense of self, of your amazing power to heal yourself and shake off those clouded thoughts. Over the years I've leant on the power of positive affirmations: speaking things into existence, and watching them become real in some shape or form. Affirmations have helped me feel comfortable with communicating my needs,

7

wants, fears and hopes. I want you to speak your wellness needs into existence while reading this book. At the end of each chapter, in the Practice Pages, I want you to hold yourself accountable, taking from my words whatever you can and building a plan.

I hope this book helps spark your curiosity about who you really are – not how you portray yourself to be, or even who everyone else wants you to be – and how magical, brilliant and powerful that real version of you is. I hope this book encourages you to say yes when you want to, but also to say no when you wish to. I hope this book slowly but surely helps you to heal parts of you that are hurting and find joy in the mundane everyday moments of life. I hope this book shows you that there is another way to be, if you are currently looking for another path.

RULES OF READING

I know I've spent a long time saying that your route to calming your mind and healing is your own personal journey. However, to get the most out of this book there are four rules to bear in mind (and, wonderfully, they can be applied to your life in general too):

1. STOP AND SLOW DOWN

Society has made this the hardest thing of all to achieve. However, whenever you're reading, I would like you to use that time as an opportunity to be still and slow down. To do that, you need to eliminate your biggest distractions. It could be your phone: if you can't turn it off, at least turn it over. It could be your home: if you're able to find a spot or a time when you won't be disturbed, do that, or simply step outside and read in your nearest green space, or on the stairwell. Welcoming a little bit of stillness into your life will enable you to hear what your body needs. When you press Pause, you are able to notice the parts of you that have been neglected and thus create space for your true feelings to reveal themselves. And then the work can begin to create real, tangible change.

2. BELIEVE THAT HEALING IS EMPOWERING

OK, I promise I'm not demanding, but I'm going to need you to believe 100 per cent that it is possible for you to heal. That a life with better mental health is achievable for you. That you are worthy of help and kindness. That a few steps

9

towards a better you constitute the best decision you'll ever make. Sometimes we have to motivate ourselves to try something new, even though it can be scary and overwhelming. However, that little spark of confidence to try it will embolden you on this journey and help create a stronger you. I learnt that it was empowering for me to carve out time in my busy life in order to actively heal; to reject what society had told me about my body and brain, and do some digging that led to approaches that made me feel reconnected, grounded and, ultimately, happier.

3. FACE YOUR FEARS

I really like the person I am now: a woman full of energy, truth and innate wisdom. However, if I'm honest, getting to this point wasn't always a comfortable or easy journey. To face yourself, when you've been running from yourself for so long (without always realising it), is challenging, to say the least. Often it can feel as if you are at war with yourself, can't it? Your mind is racing, but you don't know how to slow it down. But by being honest with yourself, the truth you've been hiding and the fears you've ignored will help you step into the light – and you deserve to see yourself shine.

4. GET INTO THE HABIT OF WRITING THINGS DOWN

Self-reflection is a powerful tool that, over time, can enable us to harness our emotional intelligence. When we stop to reflect and tap into how we feel, our awareness grows and the connection we have with ourselves becomes deeper. Use the Practice Pages at the end of each chapter to take a breather and write or draw whatever you feel. Feel no judgement or attachment about whatever comes out – simply let it flow and acknowledge it.

CHAPTER 1

GETTING TO KNOW YOU

Many of us are still operating from a place of people-pleasing and seeking outside validation for our lives, which can massively affect our sense of self. Combine that with the low confidence we may be feeling and a lack of self-care on top, and is it any wonder we feel so off-balance at times? 'Intersectionality' – a term created by the lawyer and civil-rights advocate Dr Kimberlé Crenshaw – helps us understand the nuances of people. It describes how social categories, such as race, class and gender, all overlap and 'intersect' and how they can affect the experiences we have and the prejudices we may face.

Intersectionality plays a huge part in the way a marginalised person navigates his or her way through daily life. Existing in a body that is already believed to be 'less than' in society, and subject to unfair scrutiny, can wreak havoc on someone's emotional well-being and their ability to enjoy a fulfilled life. For many Black, brown and indigenous people there is a daily and exhausting battle against systemic racial bias, via institutions that are malignant with systematic racism, as well as constant discrimination and stereotypes. There is also the added weight of generational expectations: the pressure to succeed, to be the first in your family, to provide for your family, and so on.

Studies show that there is a strong link between racism and stress. For many Black and brown people, their racial trauma can often be misdiagnosed or ignored by qualified professionals – leading to more depression, chronic stress and other symptoms that resemble post-traumatic stress disorder (PTSD). It's important to be able to bring your full self on the journey to healing and calming your mind. You have to believe that you are important, and that other people should respect what makes you *you*, if they are going to guide you through your healing. Learning how to self-advocate and have autonomy over your body is the first step in recognising what self-care looks like for you.

WHO THE FUCK ARE YOU?

There are tons of reasons tons of reasons why we struggle to know who we are, at a profound level. It could be a tough upbringing, a difficult childhood or peer pressure from society and culture. Instead of discovering all these wonderful and weird things that make us *us*, we often become who others have told us we are, and who we should be. We listen to the voice that tells us we are not enough; or that we should change a part of ourselves in order to be liked more and fit in better. Conforming is part of the process during our teenage years – we admire our friends and have countless celebrity crushes, and we want to pick and borrow part of their personality or style as our own. But that pressure to be someone else has increased over the years, following the overuse of social media, making the transition from impressionable teenager to a seemingly self-sufficient adult ever harder. Even for those of us who transition through that phase and reach our early twenties with a greater sense of self, in truth we actually don't know who the fuck we are. We've all been there, and it can be daunting to look in the mirror and not recognise the person looking back at you.

However, I believe this can also be a defining moment when, with renewed courage, strength and self-belief, we can begin a journey of self-discovery. When we *self-actualise* – and realise our full potential, recognising our own talents and capabilities – and believe we have the power within us to be who we are in a single moment, without placing judgement or attachment on how we feel or what we do, that's when we begin the process of knowing who we really are. To get to know ourselves, we must explore all facets of ourselves – even the aspects that we dislike or feel uncomfortable with. We can use the tools of *self-reflection*, *self-honesty* and *self-compassion* to connect with the parts of ourselves that we have suppressed and hidden, as well as uncovering those parts that we didn't even know were there.

— **SELF-REFLECTION:** Thinking about who you are, your character and why you do what you do.

— **SELF-HONESTY:** Holding yourself accountable, and being honest with yourself about who you are – the good, the bad and the ugly.

— **SELF-COMPASSION:** Holding no judgement or self-hate towards any realisations of yourself that you may have after self-reflection. When we are compassionate towards ourselves, we are more likely to evolve and understand who we really are.

These three processes take strength, work and a whole heap of motivation, but with consistency they can lead to self-actualisation. To really take action in our lives and create inner joy, we have to face ourselves and own up to our own bullshit, but this doesn't mean berating and over-critiquing ourselves. We can admit our faults but recognise our amazingness too! When we focus on the self, we need to do so in a compassionate way and try and hold no judgement about whatever comes up as we contemplate different parts of ourselves.

Finding out who the fuck we are means that we start from a position of pride, and begin searching for meaning. We must start to question everything and stand firm in the answers that come from those questions. We must (if we can) connect more with our heritage and ancestry. We must get creative, exploring new opportunities for ourselves – finally signing up for that class (or quitting it altogether). We must make decisions that feel right for us, and only us. Something I always tell myself, when trying to remember who I am, is: *What I like, you might hate. What I hate, you might like. What I believe to be real, you may believe to be false.* Those sentences always centre me – reminding me that I have the power to assert whatever I want. We must seek all that we are and all that we would like from life, with the belief that we can achieve anything we perceive we are worthy of. And remember: *You are worthy of it all!*

CHOOSING YOURSELF

There's a popular saying: 'You cannot pour from an empty cup.' Believe it or not, that empty cup is you. When you are empty, you often feel drained, teetering on the brink of a burnout and lacking self-love and inner peace. We often get to that point by being so much for other people, and so little for ourselves. It may sound obvious, but our lives are *ours* and are meant to be discovered and created by us alone. You have to choose yourself as much as you can, especially on this journey. You have to be a little bit selfish at times – it's good to be selfish occasionally, because then you have to focus on your needs and your wants, and make time for yourself just as you make time for everyone else.

It's important to remember that while others can influence our experiences and perspectives, they can only do so if we want them to, and if we let them. Take, for instance, love. I contributed my understanding of the way I love – and the way I want to be loved – to my boyfriend; however, he did not walk me down that road, but simply held my hand as I walked myself. As adults, we make the decisions and steer ourselves down whatever path we believe is right for us, and even though we may not have had much say as children, in the present moment we do have a say. Our voices matter, and we deserve to be heard. We have to be the ones in the driving seat, even if we're being supported. Ultimately only *you* can make decisions for you.

Sometimes the decision we make may be the wrong one – that's natural; it's called making mistakes, and we do make them. By putting yourself back in the driving seat of your life, you may make a wrong turn into a situation that you find difficult and challenging. However, I feel that adds to the variety in our lives, and is much better than being told exactly which path to take to avoid those challenges and difficulties, and knowing what the outcome will be at the end. How boring is that? Living the life you choose is empowering, and it only needs to make sense to you. Granted, if you have dependants, then this view needs to be adapted, but I'm speaking of the affirming nature of choosing to do right by yourself first – being OK in your own skin, and standing tall in your shoes. If we don't choose ourselves, we are simply choosing other people, which means that we believe they are more important and deserving than we are. We cannot hold other people up, to the detriment of ourselves; and it's imperative that we have the confidence and self-assurance to know when it's time to choose ourselves. Sometimes it's good to put yourself first and keep your own cup full.

UNPICKING YOUR CHILDHOOD

Our core self is also known as our true self, or most authentic self. The inner wisdom that we have inside us often derives from our early childhood experiences. We are who we are because of our parents, their childhoods, and so on. It is our history. This includes the way our parents or guardians raised us, and the wider environment in which we grew up: what was our home life like – were we encouraged, and did we do activities?

If a traumatic event happened early on in your life, such as a fatal accident, a death or abuse, this takes a massive toll on your brain, as a child. There are statistics to support the theory that the period of infancy from newborn to three years old is the most vital stage of human life. As reports from Unicef and the Centre for Educational Neuroscience show, the first three years of life are the most important in shaping a child's brain architecture, providing the base for the brain's functioning throughout life.[*] What we experience in our childhood really

---

[*] https://www.unicef.org/ffl/03/; http://www.educationalneuro science.org.uk/resources/neuromyth-or-neurofact/most-learning-happens-in-the-first-3-years/

shapes the adults we become. It forms the root of many of our values, the making of our identity and the relationships we seek out. It influences our interpersonal skills: how we love, and how we fight.

Some of us may feel resentment and shame about our childhoods and the ways in which we experienced family life, maybe due to domestic violence, individual cultural practices or living away from our natural home in foster or residential care. However, we are more than capable of unlearning, relearning and 'parenting' ourselves. As adults we are responsible for our own self-development and healing – and this includes unlearning toxic beliefs and thought patterns that we may have been taught in our familial environments as children. For personal transformation, we also need to unlearn any out-of-date and potentially harmful coping mechanisms that we may have developed due to trauma, and then teach ourselves how to manage our emotions in a safe and healthy way. All of this unlearning and relearning is actually a parenting of ourselves – finding ways and tools that benefit us and bring us greater peace.

FINDING SELF-FULFILMENT

One of the most exciting and yet difficult parts of being an adult is the intentional and conscious exploration of the self – basically, how we get to know ourselves better. As adults (even though we may not feel as if we are adults), we have the ability to discover for ourselves and redefine who we are; the capacity to realise our desires and ambitions and make them real. For some people, this is thrilling and invigorating; for others, it is anxiety-inducing and terrifying. It takes courage and vulnerability to find who we are, especially while navigating life and the highs and lows of adulthood. Even so, if we don't self-actualise and realise our full potential, we fail to acknowledge our true selves, our innate power and the capability within ourselves to live a centred and balanced life – which, I may add, we *absolutely* deserve.

When we journey towards self-fulfilment, really digging at the things we want to achieve – going on that trip, learning a new skill, creating healthy boundaries – we don't simply find it in blessings and joyous moments; we also need to explore the darker, more difficult aspects of ourselves. This is called 'shadow work' – it is a practice to help us find true joy and peace in life. It helps us dig into the dark parts of ourselves that we have failed to recognise, or tried very hard to hide. Deep in our murky corners we can find the ways in which we self-sabotage and self-betray: the times we said no to a wonderful new opportunity because we were scared, and it would have taken us out of our comfort zone. Or even the funny childhood quirks that we used to have, but were shamed for and, as a result, have buried deep within us. Getting to know ourselves – the real *you* – is an honour that we often deny ourselves because we are afraid of what we will find.

WHAT MAKES YOU *YOU*?

There are so many things that make us who we are. We could take it back to our childhood hobbies, or one standout teacher who made us believe we could do anything. To the traditional Sunday dinner we had every week without fail; or the 'cry-your-heart-out' CD that we reach for when going through heartbreak. Or maybe that's just me? At the heart of what makes us is our cultural heritage and our ancestral lineage. Depending on your childhood and how close to your cultural identity you were raised – namely, depending on your nationality, ethnicity and religion – that broadly includes a social group with its own distinct culture. This may be something you engage and connect with regularly (through food, music or religion) or not. However, these areas of us can also be forgotten and become subconscious parts of our lives, if they were pushed on us too hard, resulting in resentment and a sense of disconnection.

It has taken me years to learn who I am, including what my blackness looks like for me. And guess what? I am still learning, and I don't think learning ever ends. We can evolve and transform as many times as we need to, and I think that's beautiful. Food, music and history are three ways that I personally connect to my heritage and self-define what it means to be a British mixed-race Black woman. Growing up, I never had a relationship with my father so I was never taught about my Caribbean heritage and the lived experience of my ancestors. It wasn't until 2016 that I took it upon myself to read books on Caribbean and African history, as well as question the teachings around Black culture, history and people that I learnt in school. Our experience is so vast, as we are multi-faceted, and not one single thing. However, there are a lot of harmful stereotypes that surround Black people. To add to that, when you are mixed-race, your connection to your blackness may come with a sense of added confusion and lack of belonging. I turn to a number of practices such as writing and talking to my ancestors, as well as eating traditional Caribbean food, which allows me to reflect upon my lineage and feel the history of my people through every word and in every bite.

Abraham Maslow's Hierarchy of Needs is a theory and exercise created to explain our motivations. Maslow's hierarchy is famously drawn as a pyramid, with our most basic needs at the bottom (food, water, rest and warmth), gradually progressing to another set of needs that have to be met (such as safety), before getting into the really deep stuff that focuses on our psychological and social needs (such as community, love, friendships and social groups). At the top of the pyramid is 'self-actualisation' – which means that you realise who you are, have full knowledge of what you are capable of doing, are self-aware and less concerned with others and more with fulfilling your own potential. There is so much power, and endless opportunities for self-exploration, when we begin the process of finding out who we are. What makes us *us* is complicated by the fact that so many experiences impact on our sense of ourselves, but at the same time it is also very simple: what makes us *us* is everything we are, everything we are not, and the freedom to discover it all.

MAKING TIME FOR *YOU* – SELF-CARE

Self-care is a practice. Let me repeat that: *self-care is a practice*. It is a routine and a habit that you develop, because it is something that you actively have to work on in order to protect your well-being and happiness, particularly if you suffer from stress. So often self-care is pitched as something for the moment – something instant, for *now*. However, I specifically refer to it as a practice and routine because over time you will develop the habit of making self-care regular, scheduling it into your day-to-day life so that it becomes a mainstay, and not an optional way of taking care of yourself.

Self-care is defined by you, and its routines are very much up to you. What makes you feel calm, connected and centred may completely irritate, distract and imbalance someone else. That's the beauty of being different. I learnt this when I told a friend that the favourite part of my self-care routine was massage, although she couldn't stand the thought of being touched intimately. You really do have to find out what works for you. But self-care routines aren't always about diving into an indulgence or something luxurious. Although I wish all self-care routines could involve massages and face masks, sometimes we need more tangible tools and practices that serve our greater good in the moment or will benefit us in the long run.

Self-care can be about saying no to a request for your time and presence. It can be about creating boundaries around yourself, and even having difficult conversations with people. Often self-care is pitched as something immediate – an instant solution for whatever you're going through right now – but try to remember it as a habit that you need to build. Something that, with time, will be your saving grace later on.

Below is a list of possible self-care routines and practices to aid your reactive and proactive well-being. It is by no means exhaustive, but I believe there are a few ideas there for everyone.

28

SELF-CARE IDEAS

SLEEP: Make sure you're getting between seven and eight hours' sleep, if you can. Sleep is vital to the way you maintain your physical and mental health.

SWITCH OFF: Give yourself a cut-off point in the evening when you will be off your phone. Leave it in another room before you go to bed, so that it doesn't affect point number one.

HYDRATE: Drink water regularly throughout the day. It's vital for your physical health, supporting your body's temperature, delivering nutrients to your cells and keeping your organs functioning.

BREATHE: Breathe in. Breathe out. Repeat! It's that simple. Your breath is one of your most powerful tools for stress regulation, calming your nervous system and giving you new energy. Make your breaths intentional at least three or four times a day. Breathe into every part of your body.

THINK IT OVER: We've all been there: by impulse we've said yes too soon, or something unkind in the heat of the moment. Give yourself time to think before making decisions. Contrary to the culture of immediacy, you don't need to respond to things straight away.

CREATE SPACE: Implement boundaries and honour them. Ask yourself: 'What am I willing to put up with?' What's OK for you and what's not? How do you want, and deserve, to be treated? Create a sanctuary in your surroundings too. It's hard to find calm in chaos – so tidy your room, frame that picture or buy a plant.

BUDGET: Be aware of your financial situation as much as you can. Burying your head in the sand about the state of your bank balance will lead to financial struggles down the line.

GO OUTSIDE: Get out of the house and connect with the green spaces that your town or city has to offer, and with nature, when you can. I'm not saying hug a tree; well, I am – go and hug one.

Studies show that a meaningful relationship with nature can improve our mental health so much.

INVEST IN *YOU*: Whether it's a new hobby or learning a new skill, do something that brings value to your life creatively. You are worth it, and you can learn something new.

SHOW GRATITUDE: Saying 'Thank you' goes a long way. Showing your appreciation for others is an act of kindness. I personally believe it boosts your vibration levels and makes you feel good.

HOLD YOURSELF ACCOUNTABLE: Look, no one is perfect, and we *all* fuck up from time to time and, believe me, that's OK. But a big lesson in self-care is making sure you're doing the necessary work. That involves you being really honest with yourself, and saying sorry when you're in the wrong. It also means setting personal milestones, and celebrating when you reach your goals. Remember I said that it's about creating a practice and habit.

> **REST:** Burning out is not fun, cool or productive. Sometimes doing nothing is doing something.

MAKING TIME FOR *YOU* – SELF-DISCOVERY

Self-care and self-discovery overlap a little, as the main focus is always you. However, self-discovery allows you to dig a little deeper – consider it your own personal mission to get to the top of Maslow's Hierarchy of Needs, where you will gain far more insight into your own character and have full knowledge of your abilities and feelings. Quite often spiritual practices are about deepening your connection to your self, and exploring parts of yourself that may have been neglected or locked away, due to shame or past trauma. In order to get to know who we are and discover our full selves, we must become curious in our thoughts and our reactions, and introduce healthy habits into our daily routines.

Below is a list of possible self-discovery routines to introduce into your day-to-day life. The aim is that they help you to self-actualise and realise your full potential.

SELF-DISCOVERY IDEAS

JOURNALING: By writing down your morning thoughts, or taking the time to self-reflect and note how you feel at the end of the day, you will be able to see a pattern in your emotions and behaviour, and any subconscious beliefs that you may hold. Our minds are often filled with so much chaos, from our racing thoughts, that it's hard to focus on and pay attention to the present. By putting pen to paper you are trying to slow those thoughts down, bring calm in and process your feelings. This will lead to greater self-awareness.

MEDITATION: Meditation doesn't have to mean sitting on the floor surrounded by candles and incense, with your hands on your knees, humming. It can simply be a few moments in which you close your eyes, disconnect from everything around you and just *breathe* (see Breathwork on page 84). Contrary to popular belief, you can meditate anywhere – while sitting on the bus or underground train, when you pop to the shops or when you go around your block for a short walk. Look at meditation as eliminating the cobwebs: when you meditate, you intentionally centre and create space inside yourself, feeling connected to your body and holding space for yourself.

TAROT-CARD READING: This is the centuries-old practice of using Tarot cards to gain insight into the past, present or future by formulating a question, then drawing and interpreting the cards. I've found that Tarot can challenge me, make me think, encourage self-awareness and self-accountability. It's a spiritual practice that can make you feel closer to yourself, the Divine, God or the universe – whatever name resonates with you. Tarot is simply a tool that can expand your mind and plant a seed of love, healing and trust inside you.

CREATIVITY: Being creative is good for the soul and something that, as adults, we often forget how to do. Getting creative allows us to connect with our inner child, which in turn creates opportunities for healing and growth. When we create, we release, feel joy and relax, releasing those feel-good hormones such as serotonin, dopamine and oxytocin that spur us on and give us positive feelings. Creativity may be different for everyone, but my own go-tos are painting and making a memory book full of photos. Being creative without desiring a particular outcome, and doing it purely for yourself, is so therapeutic. I sometimes paint whatever is in my head and, when I feel like stopping, I do. Admittedly there are about seventeen half-finished paintings stuffed in my cupboards, but who cares? Not everything needs to be finished, perfect or capitalised upon. Sometimes just have fun, and let it be whatever it needs to be.

PRACTICE PAGES

You've arrived at your first set of practice pages. I've spoken enough about self-care and self-discovery. Redraw the Maslow Hierarchy of Needs for yourself. Take one aspect from all the text in this chapter to work on. This space is yours to compress all you've read so far and start building your own self-care toolbox.

....

....

....

....

....

....

....

....

....

....

....

PRACTICE PAGES

....
....
....
....
....
....
....
....
....
....
....
....
....
....
....
....
....

PRACTICE PAGES

....

....

....

....

....

....

....

....

....

....

....

....

....

....

....

....

CHAPTER 2

EVERYTHING IS CONNECTED

Before we get to the practice of detangling what goes on in our heads, we absolutely must know our bodies at a deeper level. For a long time the industry of wellness, health and fitness focused solely on how our bodies looked, what size of jeans we could squeeze into, which latest food trend we should eat and how far we could physically push ourselves in the gym. It led us to believe that the perfect size or fad diet would make us feel good, which for me has never been further from the truth. This was all results-based, rather than connecting with our feelings and our bodies. To combat that, we need to bring together our mind, body and soul. A transformational approach to wellness exists when the focus is on uniting body, mind and soul for a stronger connection to our emotional and mental health.

KNOWING YOUR BODY

There is such a profound connection between our minds (what we think), our bodies (what we feel) and our soul (the spiritual part of us, the bit that works on energy). All these aspects combined build up a special type of map/memory for our bodies, and a new way of understanding how to process them. Think about it. Have you ever been really angry, but held that feeling of anger in and it caused you pain? I know this feeling all too well, because if I don't honour my anger and frustration, releasing them from my body, I end up with an uncomfortable pain in my neck and feet, because that's where my tension is stored.

Taking it back to the map I just spoke of, how we feel, how we think and what we do about it can manifest itself in our bodies, leaving imprints such as spotty skin, thin hair, deeper physical illness or full-on exhaustion. We have to realise – sometimes the hard way – that we aren't simply a set of bones covered in muscles and skin, walking, talking and being. We are complex souls with many layers, and for us to truly thrive, we need to understand how our bodies are wired, in order to contribute to a better ecosystem of health. How do we feel when X happens? How does our body react when Y occurs? Have you ever felt your shoulders and jaw tense when you're around someone who makes you feel uncomfortable? And have you recognised the tiredness that you feel in every part of your body when you have been socialising for too long? These bodily responses are showing you what needs tending to – on a physical, mental and spiritual level – and you shouldn't ignore them.

If you have periods, your monthly cycle can also affect you physically, not just with bleeding and cramps, but with brain-fog too! I find that my levels of serotonin – the chemical that controls mood – drop, and I feel less sharp and way more sluggish and flat. I often find that I can't string a complete sentence together and want to hibernate away from the world. Figuring out your own body's map requires you to slow down a little and tune into how you feel in mind, body and soul. Only then can you begin to honour those feelings properly, by working to nourish them and heal yourself of the regular ills that pain you. You can tie into that some fun and self-care too. Go back to the list of Self-Care Ideas on page 29 and give yourself a reward to help that feeling along. Is it sleep, a home-cooked meal, a long bath, an energising boxing class or a loud scream into a pillow that you need? Listen to your body and then take action.

KNOWING WHERE YOU COME FROM

Likewise, you need to understand your childhood, and how that influences your behaviour. Our identity has a deep impact on our overall well-being, and in order to feel whole, we need to understand where we've come from and how that can impact upon the person we are today; we need to locate our sources of trauma and anxiety and, ultimately, our approach to healing. Learning about our heritage and history is a starting point to knowing who we are – not only because our ancestral truth is really interesting, but also because it can give us a sense of belonging, especially for those of us who have experienced a feeling of disconnection. In 2016 I began exploring what it means to be a Black mixed-race woman in Britain. My dad is from St Vincent's and my mum is British, and I grew up in High Wycombe in Buckinghamshire. At that time in my life I felt as if I needed to create a greater sense of kinship and community, and relate to people who looked like me.

I started to read more actively about Black history and our accomplishments in the world. There are parts of Black history that are deeply traumatising. The legacy and impact of slavery affects Black and brown people in multiple ways today, and is largely upheld in our institutions. As a result we need to combat that feeling of displacement and come home - connecting to our innate spiritual compass. This could be done through yearly holidays or pilgrimages to your ancestral home; by changing your name to dissociate yourself from your 'slave name'; or simply by reading more books or seeing more documentaries on where you have come from. Coming home to ourselves, through our culture, is an opportunity to reclaim the glorious parts of our history, which were buried within Western society and the institutions that I speak of.

Generally education has been 'white-washed' to erase the contribution that Black and brown people have made to Britain. The same goes for other indigenous cultures. Knowledge is power, and when we learn who we are, how powerful we are and have the spiritual belief that our ancestors are with us – next to us, and inside us, right now – we are able to feel supported and loved, and to move towards a sense of wholeness that we were missing. When we feel strong and grounded in our identities, we have more confidence and tangible ways to advocate ourselves and honour different parts of us. This could be done through food, prayer, physical community, traditions, celebrations or practices and history. You should honour your culture and connect to it in a way that feels right and true for you.

TRUSTING YOUR GUT

Our intuition – the ability to understand or know something, based on feelings, rather than facts – is something we have probably all experienced throughout our lives. It is an innate feeling that sometimes we can't quite explain, but when that feeling comes, it is hard to ignore it; and yet so many of us have been programmed to disregard it. There are times when we are so full of emotion and inner turmoil that we may not be able to feel our intuition strongly enough. Or if we have experienced a trauma that has made us question whether we can trust ourselves, or the decisions we make, we may not listen to our gut. I'll talk about trauma more in a later chapter, but huge parts of trauma are shame and blame. It's so easy to blame ourselves for the things that have happened to us; and it is even easier to hold on and refuse to forgive ourselves for past mistakes or mishaps because we don't believe we are deserving of forgiveness. Let me tell you: you are!

We're naturally intuitive beings, but we have lost our connection to our gut because we're living in an age of information and misinformation; we over-think and have limited self-belief, which can lead to depression and anxiety and greatly compromise our intuition. I think the culture of working hard, and hustling, has made this more difficult too. Capitalism has taught us that if we aren't grinding or working towards something, then we are failures, doomed to a life of no fulfilment or happiness. We have been conditioned to believe that without working ourselves to the bone, we won't be able to succeed – but this is false. These beliefs are fear-based and are rooted in our society as a way to keep us bound to a system that does not work. These systems are the ones making us ill, depressed and stressed and it's about time this changed.

Our intuition gets suppressed or pushed to the side because we are operating from a place of fear – fear of failure, fear of loss, fear of falling behind – and so we remain on the hamster wheel, hoping that one day we'll wake up and everything will be as right as rain. Unfortunately, for most of us, that's not how it goes. When we tap into ourselves and pay attention to what's really going on, we are able to honour the calling and purpose of our lives. Our intuition enables us to *select* our choices, instead of allowing our programming to do it for us. Trusting our gut takes time and patience, and really comes back to how well we know ourselves and how stable and confident we feel about who we are.

THE SEVEN DIMENSIONS

Before I knew what the Seven Dimensions were, I did know that we are all products of our environment – remember the importance of where you get your sense of worth and identity from – and that, as powerful human beings, our thoughts are connected to our feelings, and our feelings can manifest themselves in our body. I knew that if I wanted to start to feel better about myself, whole-istically and holistically, I needed to begin viewing myself as a full person and healing myself as a full person. I needed to identify all the interlinking parts that contribute to my overall wellness. Identifying and remedying these areas would bring me greater balance in life and a better understanding of what I needed in order to nurture and work on myself and heal.

The Seven Dimensions are a multifaceted view of life. This includes our emotional, spiritual, physical, environmental, social, intellectual and vocational needs. Imagine the Seven Dimensions as a map, like the underground system or the solar system – except that it's all interlinked and connected inside you, alongside your anatomy. The connection between the mind and the body is so strong that mental and physical states feed into each other, with both positive and negative influences. Feelings depend on thoughts, and both determine our attitudes and actions. Throughout life, in all our experiences (whether good or bad), we come to learn that we hold the reins of our lives in our own hands and can create whatever we believe we are worthy of. Our feelings don't actually depend on *what* is happening to us, but rather on our interpretations and reactions to what is happening to us.

The mind–body connection, in one simple word, represents 'duality', and duality exists in multiple forms all around us: Light and Dark, Yin and Yang, Sun and Moon, Love and Fear. We don't exist in a world that is one or the other; we exist in a grey area, a spectrum of millions and millions of energetic vibrations that change and adapt every millisecond.

I   EMOTIONAL WELLNESS

This relates to the emotional quality that someone has, and their sense of self. Your emotional well-being is determined by many factors, including trauma, illness, socio-economic factors and the ability to self-soothe and self-regulate. Emotional well-being is also linked to the way someone copes with life and maintains their relationships with self and with others.

IDENTIFYING IT

When it comes to our emotional needs, we often fall short of actually identifying them because of our impacted sense of self. For instance, as children we may have experienced neglect or trauma, and as adults we may have experienced a difficult relationship or a chronic illness. We are all products of our environment – as children, we navigate through whatever our parents and their careers project onto us, and the lessons they have taught us, either consciously or subconsciously. We arrive at adulthood with perceptions of the world, which we then realise that we need to redefine and re-perceive for ourselves. This takes work and can be extremely difficult, because we don't always have the tools to know how to do so. We identify our emotional needs by acknowledging how we respond to ourselves and others; by paying attention to the thoughts we have about ourselves and our life experiences; by recognising whether we are comfortable with who we are, our needs and the boundaries we need to adhere to; as well as by taking the time to explore the experiences we have been through, and whether or not they have impacted on the way we feel about ourselves.

ASK YOURSELF

1. Am I able to express my emotions freely?

2. When I get [insert emotion], can I recognise it, do I understand why I am feeling this way, and am I OK with this feeling?

3. Can I be truly honest with myself?

REMEDYING IT

After you bring awareness to your emotional well-being, you are able to change, adapt, evolve, grow and move forward. Changing how we respond and face ourselves can be tough. As a society, we often bury our heads in the ground and remain emotionally closed off and stagnant because it feels easier and, subconsciously, it's where we feel most comfortable. There needs to be a willingness to choose yourself over and over again, and delve deep into your core and become who you are, without anyone else's influence. Emotional intelligence takes unlearning and relearning, and it is constant – a conscious decision that we make every day to 'do better'. However, don't fall into the trap of constant self-improvement, because this can actually be detrimental to your overall well-being. I used to dedicate too much time to healing, which resulted in a lack of creativity, fun and social aspects. Sometimes to 'do better' means to rest, take a day off and say no.

TRY TO

- Be still and silent so that you can recognise your emotions.

- Sit with how you feel – even if it's uncomfortable; explore the meaning behind the feeling.

- Remind yourself that feelings are fleeting and will eventually pass.

---

2 SPIRITUAL WELLNESS

The spiritual dimension of wellness relates to the expansion of your purpose and finding a deeper meaning of life, helping you to go through life with an overall positive mindset. It is about connecting to a set of beliefs, values and principles that help guide you through adulthood, and relate to others better too. The spiritual dimension enables the capacity for self-exploration, which can often lead to a sense of peace and harmony.

IDENTIFYING IT

We identify our spiritual well-being by exploring what it means to be alive, and our view on religion, creation and all that is, to recognise whether we believe in something bigger than 'us'. Some people's spiritual beliefs come from religion, while others decide to take a different route, but I think it is really important to be aware of the path you have chosen vs a path that someone else chose for you. It's OK if your spiritual beliefs change throughout your life – that's the beauty of your evolution. To be spiritual could mean being connected to religion, although I think we sometimes discount something else that guides us – our gut. Our intuition is one of our greatest gifts, but we are often told in covert ways to ignore it. Intuition is our portal to innate knowing and a deep trust of self, coupled with the motivation and inspiration to find a deeper meaning for existence – that is one of our superpowers, if you ask me.

ASK YOURSELF

1. Do I believe in God, a higher power or something bigger than myself?

2. Do I view my life as meaningful?

3. Do I know my values and beliefs, and do I understand the 'why' behind them?

REMEDYING IT

After we identify and bring awareness to our spiritual well-being, we are able to truly discover the beauty in searching for the meaning behind our thoughts, decisions and actions. Spirituality is definitely self-defined, but it sits within a framework of understanding that we really are the masters of our own lives.

TRY TO

- Explore the spectrum of spirituality, and look for signs in things all around you.

- Take the time to recognise your intuition, trust it and listen.

- Start a new practice that will allow you to connect with your body and grow.

3 PHYSICAL WELLNESS

The physical dimension of well-being relates to the care and attention we give our bodies to support it in the best possible way. This may be through nutrition, movement, sleep and medical care. Looking after your physical side also means having an awareness of your need for physical intervention on your body, such as massage and reflexology– where different amounts of pressure are applied to your feet and hands. Being in tune with your physical self, and any bodily changes that you have, will enable you to meet your lifelong needs more easily.

IDENTIFYING IT

For some people the physical aspect of wellness is extremely easy, while others really struggle, due to the society we live in and its obsession with appearance. There is so much emphasis on the physical because that is where the money is – hello, capitalism! The diet and fitness industries are both worth millions of pounds. The ways we are told that we aren't good enough usually centre on what we look like. Our physical well-being, however, is so much more than simply our body weight and size – it's about how connected we feel to our bodies, the thoughts we have around the body we inhabit, and how we take care of that body. It's about making sure we go to the doctor if we have a persistent issue; ensuring we have an eating and fitness regime that works for our individual body needs; and not being shamed into thinking it's too much or not enough.

ASK YOURSELF

1. How do I feel about my body? Do I feel as if it's mine, and do I like the body I'm in?

2. Do I enjoy sex, and when was the last time I had a sexual health check?

3. Do I enjoy food; do I know when I'm hungry and when I'm full?

REMEDYING IT

After we identify and bring awareness to our physical well-being, we are then able to reconnect to our bodies, show them compassion and begin to unlearn the programming we have experienced about the importance of our exterior. We must explore our relationships to food and exercise, and be totally honest about the way the world has impacted on our intuitive wisdom with regard to eating, movement generally and appreciating and understanding our own body. Trauma and suppressed emotions are held within our bodies, mainly in the lower back, the bottom of the skull and the lower belly, for those of us with wombs. Pent-up energy will remain inside us, so we need to be aware of what emotions our bodies could be carrying.

TRY TO

- Find a form of exercise that you actually enjoy, and commit to a schedule of making it a habit.

- Give yourself enough time in your day to prepare and cook a balanced meal that you like.

- Remember that the health-and-fitness industry has contributed to the image of what a 'healthy' body is – ignore it, and know your own body.

---

4 ENVIRONMENTAL WELLNESS

This dimension relates to the global environment that we live in, as well as our personal homes. We have a responsibility to nature to be considerate in our consumption on this Earth, and to play our part in protecting and conserving it for future generations. Closer to home, our environmental wellness means making sure that the rooms you live in are clean, clutter-free and hygienic, because dirt and chaos can have a knock-on effect on physical wellness. Caring for both the global and personal environment is essential, as we need to protect what we have and maintain spaces that contribute to our energy, mood and overall sense of calm.

IDENTIFYING IT

Now, more than ever, we must hold ourselves accountable for the climate crisis: our oceans are rising, temperatures are changing drastically and there is excessive pollution in our skies. Heavy pollution and constant carbon emissions can cause fatal hormone imbalances and mood disorders, and can disturb our respiratory and circulatory systems. While I don't believe that climate change is all down to society, I do think capitalism and huge corporations have played a role in the Earth's demise. We all have to show and practise more care, love and protection towards this wonderful planet.

ASK YOURSELF

1. What can I do to play my part in contributing to protecting the planet?

2. Can I relax fully in my home?

3. How can I better connect with nature?

REMEDYING IT

After we bring awareness to this dimension we can focus on how our natural environment - meaning the spaces we find ourselves in everyday such as our homes, our workspaces, or our vehicles - impacts our general well-being. Limiting the negative impact they can have by curating these spaces to be cleaner, safer, or more harmonious is extremely beneficial. Overall it shows you have respect for your surroundings, you can be less distracted, and you want to create a space that has a positive impact on your day to day.

TRY TO

- Advocate better and safer living conditions for all.

- Make conscious choices that will protect the long-term existence of the planet.

- Create a living and work space that support your well-being and your emotions.

---

5 SOCIAL WELLNESS

The social dimension relates to connection and belonging: it's all about the range and quality of the relationships we have – whether it be to our family, our friends or the community we belong to – and how we interact with them. The social aspect of looking after ourselves relies on us forming a supportive network of people around us, and on developing the capacity to nurture positive relationships with others.

IDENTIFYING IT

We cannot navigate life alone. It is in our human nature to attach ourselves to, and depend upon, other people. A guiding principle of this, I believe, is love. The well-known Igbo proverb 'It takes a village' springs to mind here. In many African and indigenous cultures, entire villages and communities of neighbours chip in to welcome and raise a newborn baby, signing up to support that child in a ton of ways, teaching them very early on the importance of community. We can identify our social well-being by how emotionally connected and invested in others we are, and how supported we feel by family, friends and the wider community or our support network. For some people, having a close family isn't an option or important, and they lean on friendships and their community instead. It's important to note how much your own personality type – whether you are an introvert, shy, quiet and reserved person, or an extrovert, outgoing, socially confident and forward person – is a deciding factor in defining how you meet your social needs. You may, of course, be both extrovert and introvert at any one time.

REMEDYING IT

After we identify and bring awareness to this dimension, we are able to address, change and nurture the relationships in our lives. The social dimension of well-being can actually be really hard for people to work on, because it is directly impacted by our emotional well-being, past trauma and life experiences. Some people are closed off and struggle to rely on others because of their past, while other people may not wish to come across as 'needy' or 'dependent'. Developing healthy and satisfying relationships demands vulnerability, which can often remind people of pain, abandonment and rejection, thus creating a feeling of separateness. We work on our social selves by recognising our need for community or friendship, and by connecting to the way we feel about our relationships and being honest about those emotions.

TRY TO

- Effectively communicate your needs to others, and be receptive to their needs too.

- Have an inclusive community of peers and friends around you.

- Do a new cultural activity, to bring new relationships into your life.

---

6 INTELLECTUAL WELLNESS

The intellectual dimension of well-being relates to leading your life with a curious and open mind, and engaging in stimulating activities and conversations that challenge you. The intellectual parts of us need expansion and expression in order to gain more knowledge about ourselves, others and society as a whole, and to gain new experiences too. You can boost your brain power through a number of creative outlets, such as painting, drawing, dancing, reading or even doing a crossword puzzle.

IDENTIFYING IT

Our thoughts are extremely powerful and, when left to their own devices, can cause anxiety and catastrophic thinking. Just as we do with babies and infants, in adulthood we have to continue to nurture what is going on in our brains. We need to be open to learning, as well as to unlearning and evolving our thinking. Continuous learning can help to raise our consciousness, which has a profound impact on the other dimensions, such as cultural and spiritual beliefs, so that they can grow as we do. Remember: thoughts are powerful and can become our reality.

ASK YOURSELF

1. Is my mind open enough to engage in conversations with a wide variety of people?

2. Do I need to develop a new hobby or skill?

3. Do I feel threatened when my thinking is challenged?

REMEDYING IT

After we identify and bring awareness to this dimension, we can start to challenge our own thought patterns and openness. Two people may have completely different ideas and beliefs, and consider them to be true. That's the beauty of life, and if we close ourselves off to this type of conversation, then we close ourselves off to learning, expanding and evolving. However, it's important that the conversations that challenge us are not harmful or detrimental to ourselves and others.

7 VOCATIONAL WELLNESS

The vocational dimension of well-being relates to personal satisfaction concerning work, and how we spend our time and our finances to help support our needs. Vocational well-being is connected to a sense of purpose through our talents, our skills and the energy we give to our community, a cause or a charity.

IDENTIFYING IT

This is the wellness dimension that I think is spoken about the least, because 'vocational well-being' means different things to different people. Ultimately it relates to our individual skill sets and what we do with them. It's important to feel enriched and enlivened through the work we do, whether that's in our careers, creating a platform on social media or volunteering at a local shelter. *If we feel good, we do good; and if we do good, we feel good.* Financial literacy is also of huge importance, as it gives us all the ability to consciously create future financial health, as well as learning how to budget and what it means to be a 'good' consumer. We can identify our vocational well-being by how much time we give ourselves to develop and participate in tasks that encourage the growth of our skills; by the energy we commit to our careers; and by establishing whether our lives are aligned with our financial situation. It is worth noting that we cannot 'financially liberate' our way out of poverty and the systemic class divide within society. Low-income families are usually very financially literate, but lack the access to appropriate living wages.

ASK YOURSELF

1. Are my skills being actively expanded and used?

2. Am I stimulated with my job?

3. How else can life be enriched and full?

REMEDYING IT

After we identify and bring awareness to this dimension, we can begin to live with greater purpose and gratification. You know that feeling of really getting your shit together and knowing that you are impacting the world in a positive way? That is what 'vocation' is all about, and we do this by taking accountability for the parts we play in our own stories, and by conscientiously adapting or redirecting our path to best serve ourselves and others. Life really is about finding what you love, then doing it as much as you can. With regard to finances, I guess we can all agree that money is a complex thing and, for many women, something we do not talk about, for fear of judgement, persecution and shame. Money is often used to rate someone's worth (or lack thereof) in society, with the rich and those who have accumulated worth being praised, while low-income workers and those who rely on government bodies for their basic survival are punished. Individual financial well-being is, of course, important. But let me be frank: we can't manifest our way out of systemic class-ism and poverty.

TRY TO

- Explore our skills and abilities so that we can understand our individual purpose.

- Consume less stuff, but experience more life.

- Ensure we schedule in time to nurture and develop our skills.

DOING YOUR OWN RESEARCH

Even with all the advice given above, and the deep dive into some ways in which you can begin to learn more about yourself and how your body relates to your mental well-being, I'd still encourage you to do some research of your own and find out what works best for you. Listen: Google really is your best friend.

I urge everyone to find their own truth and figure out things through further research – be it podcasts, books, conversations with friends or even professionals. The information is out there, if you remain open to the teachings and learning that are calling to you. It would be limiting just to take my word for everything, rather than engaging in your own intellectual wellness dimension and thinking broadly and critically, for your own good. Vitally, you can seek out qualified professionals to help you work through all this. Some aspects of what I have mentioned may reignite triggers of a negative event or remind you of past areas of trauma, and it's important to work through that with someone who is well qualified and trained. I want you to absorb this chapter in particular, with a view to exploring what I say later on.

When I began my own journey of self-discovery after feeling stressed, overwhelmed and downright unhappy for some time, I searched for meaning everywhere. And then I took that meaning and applied it to my routine: I knew it was right for me by the way my body reacted to it. I began to trust my intuition more – watching out for signals that told me to slow down, trust more or take a leap of faith and say yes. I embraced nature: the most incredible way of learning about stillness and calm, because nature remains alive during all the seasons and affects our moods and bodies differently. I always come back to the saying, 'During autumn leaves will shed, but during spring leaves will bloom.' It makes me think of how we are constantly changing and adapting. There is nothing wrong with letting go and feeling bare – maybe that's exactly what we need in order to feel full again.

PRACTICE PAGES

You've arrived at your second set of practice pages. What have you taken from this chapter on the interconnection between mind and body? How are you going to begin your journey to becoming more connected to your body or your family history? What dimension do you want to jump in and start working on?

....

....

....

....

....

....

....

....

....

....

PRACTICE PAGES

....
....
....
....
....
....
....
....
....
....
....
....
....
....
....
....

PRACTICE PAGES

....
....
....
....
....
....
....
....
....
....
....
....
....
....
....
....
....

CHAPTER 3

DETANGLING YOUR HEAD

Our heads are often noisy, over-stimulated and full of negative thoughts, which can lead to feelings of confusion, sadness, resentment and anxiety. We tend to suppress these feelings because we are ill equipped to deal with them, and instead simply put up with our minds working in overdrive. But when we do this we create blockages and pain inside our bodies, which can result in sickness, tiredness and a complete disconnection between mind, body and soul. Detangling our heads enables us to sift through our thought patterns, become aware of them and figure out which thoughts serve us and which do not. When we spend time focusing on our thoughts, we become more aware of them and learn how to control them, instead of letting them control us. Subconscious thinking leads to subconscious behaviours, which tend to be out of date (stemming from our childhoods) and can be toxic, so when we detangle our heads we are learning how to think more mindfully.

ASKING FOR HELP

If you have the means to access it, I really believe in the power of therapy and how beneficial it can be, especially if you find a therapist who really understands you.

I've had different types of therapy from the age of twenty-one: group therapy, talking therapy and Cognitive Behaviour Therapy or CBT (see below). Some were absolutely awful experiences and others were life-changing. I found group therapy too overwhelming and generic for my problems, as if a random bunch of people were trying to offload in a way that simply couldn't contain them. With talking therapy, it felt too much like storytelling for me, and I found most sessions boring and useless. And with CBT, I felt as though it was all about my symptoms and not the root cause – it was too superficial for me. But of course, personal perspectives play a part in therapy, and what I hated, other people might love, and vice versa.

Although in theory therapy should be a safe space – a place where you can feel assured you won't be discriminated against, and a place for open-ended conversation and support – that's not always the case. We can't generalise on all therapeutic care and automatically put mental support in the 'safe space' category. At times therapy can be a place that further impacts on your mental well-being, and may even be extremely hostile to you. Therapy is so individual and dependent on your own needs, and on the therapeutic or clinical framework within which your therapist or counsellor works.

Whether it's NHS-supported therapy or self-funded private sessions, the process of finding a therapist can feel daunting, because most of us don't really know where to start. I remember being twenty-one and feeling so poorly and confused within my head; after days and days of trying to muster up the courage to do something about it, I called my local GP and blurted out to the receptionist, 'I think I'm depressed' and, luckily, the process of getting some support started there. One of the biggest hurdles to benefiting from therapy is actually asking for help and advocating for yourself in the first place, and making that call or sending that email. Often we feel so low mentally that even the action of getting out of bed and brushing our teeth is too much, let alone having to tell a stranger that you feel like utter shit.

It's important to know that you don't need to feel depressed, distressed or like utter shit to seek mental-health support. Therapy can be proactive, and something you do just because it is a good way to maintain your overall well-being. Of course if you have experienced childhood trauma or a traumatic incident, then mental-health support might be imperative. However, it really is something everyone should have access to – regardless of their previous experiences. So if you're looking for a therapist or a mental-health professional, here are some points to consider.

TYPES OF THERAPY

Currently, access to mental-health services in Britain is pretty dire. Unless you are financially comfortable and can afford to see a private therapist, or come from a background that embraces liberal beliefs, where talking to other people is seen as beneficial, then you're at the mercy of the National Health Service. Waiting times for NHS mental-health support vary, but in general it takes far too long from being referred by your GP to having your first session. Most services that are supplied for free on the NHS are short-term support options (usually lasting between six and twelve sessions); they are often very focused, and are reactive types of support, rather than delving deep into your needs, as is covered in psychotherapy.

The most widely referred therapies currently available are:

1. COGNITIVE BEHAVIOUR THERAPY (CBT)

This aims to improve mental well-being by focusing on your thoughts: how you think about your life and the decisions you make, and how they can lead to unhelpful emotions and behaviours in your life. CBT has been prescribed for mental-health needs including depression, panic attacks, phobias and obsessive-compulsive disorder.

2. COUNSELLING

This is mainly conversational: where you talk with someone either one-on-one or in a group. This type of therapy encourages you to talk about your feelings and emotions to someone who will listen without passing judgement and criticism.

Private therapy options are more varied and tailored, but depend heavily on your financial circumstances, which can make the whole process of getting help a matter of privilege, and unfair. The government must do more to fund the NHS, so that mental-health treatment can be readily available for everyone, regardless of their income, social status or race; and long term, so that everyone can have the amount of support they need.

TIMELINE OF SUPPORT

Although the timeline may depend on your individual therapist, think about the length of support you would like. Is it short-term support you need – a a six-twelve week program – or something more regular, such as a scheduled weekly check-in? Do you simply want to talk to someone or do you need coping strategies? Consider this when trying to find the correct support for you.

FINDING THE 'RIGHT' THERAPIST

If you would like support on the NHS, calling your local doctor is a great place to start, because NHS support differs from borough to borough, and from county to county. Your GP can refer you to all the resources you're entitled to through them. Another route to take is to contact a mental-health charity or organisation for support and advice, and information on how to access the right services for and near you. As you've decided on this option for yourself, there is typically a fee for the cost of your sessions. Some private therapists offer discounted rates for low-income clients, those on Jobseeker's Allowance, and students.

If you are Black, Asian or identify as a person of colour and would feel more comfortable getting support from someone within your own community and culture, or someone who looks like you, then there are platforms such as BAATN (the Black, African and Asian Therapy Network) that have an extensive list of therapists of colour; and organisations such as Black Minds Matter UK have extensive resources and contacts, which centre on your lived experience.

Once you have found the practitioner that you believe is right for you, don't hesitate to ask for more information on their method of therapy and how they tend to run their sessions. Most therapists will operate from an individual point of view, allowing you – their client – to lead the sessions, but it doesn't harm to ask, especially if you have some anxieties in that area. Ask about their qualifications; good therapists are registered with a governing body called the Professional Standards Authority (PSA). You're trusting your feelings, your time and your energies to a stranger, so make sure they are official. Remember that therapy and mental-health support are all about the relationship you have with your therapist. Be honest about the way you feel in their presence, and how what they say makes you feel. Don't be afraid to end sessions because something doesn't feel right in your gut – see, intuition really matters! – or is not as you imagined, and the therapist is not delivering the type of help and support you hoped for.

MINDFULNESS

Mindfulness is all about being fully present and engaged in what you're doing 'in the moment'. The techniques that you use to improve your mindfulness are ways to come back to the present moment, centre and connect to yourself, as well as bring awareness to how you are really feeling.

The more we practise mindfulness, the more attuned to ourselves we become, and the less likely we are to experience high levels of stress. We will also feel more present where we are, and with what we're doing, without distractions. It's something we all have the power within us to do – we just have to nurture it. I believe that a state of calm can be achieved in small, manageable ways through tasks that can be done anywhere and everywhere. Every day we can do little things to enable our nervous systems to calm down and our minds to feel they have a bit more space. Of course there are certain activities, such as resting in bed for a day, visiting a spa with a partner or going to Jamaica for a two-week holiday, that will contribute to making us feel super-chilled-out and relaxed, but these aren't always feasible – although I definitely wish they were!

Here are some mindful techniques that I recommend; as always, do the ones that work for *you*. There is no right or wrong way to be mindful, so if something makes you feel peaceful, do more of it; and if something makes you feel stressed, do less of it or don't do it at all.

I. BREATHE IN AND BREATHE OUT

Breathwork is a fairly new practice, where you take conscious control of your breathing. It can promote relaxation and ease feelings of distress. When we connect to our breath, we come back to the present and allow oxygen to reach every part of our bodies, resulting in a release of relaxing hormones. Breathing deeply – in for four counts and out for eight – can be done for time periods of one minute, five minutes or fifteen minutes for a set: whatever you feel comfortable with.

Try it now. Close your eyes and inhale deeply, imagining that with the breath you are taking in peace and light. Then exhale deeply, letting out all your heaviness and stress. When I worked in an office, which I absolutely loathed, I would do all my breathwork when I was on the toilet – proof that it could be done anywhere. It helped me to calm down greatly, and not erupt at my manager. Try it on the train, bus or even while you walk; maybe don't close your eyes when you're walking, though. You get the picture.

2. GET GROUNDED

Grounding yourself is another way to be fully present, but also to connect you to the Earth – remember the environmental dimension I was talking about in Chapter 2. When we become stressed or unsettled, that usually means we have lost stability and our connection to our bodies. To be grounded is to be in a state of alignment with your mind, body and soul, with nature and all that there is. The energy of being grounded is the energy of the entire universe, so it's in our best interests to bring that state back.

A simple grounding technique is to stand or sit. Close your eyes and feel your feet planted firmly on the ground. Shift your weight back and forth, from the balls of your feet to your heels, and even the middle section of your feet. Feeling your feet on the ground is a reminder that you are in the 'here and now' and are safe. When you repeat this, expand your senses to experience what's around you. Try it now. What can you smell? What can you hear? Repeat for as long as you need to, then notice how you feel.

3. MOVE

It's no secret that our well-being improves when we move our bodies. I'm not recommending that you jump straight into a HIIT workout, if you can't imagine doing anything worse, or even something lighter such as a yoga class, if that's your worst nightmare. Simple and everyday movement is still – guess what? – movement, whether it's a quick walk outside during your lunch break or a dance workout at home.

We need to release some of the stagnant and low-vibe energy that our bodies are holding on to. Sometimes shaking your ass and sweating it out is the perfect way to do this. When you move – be it dancing or exercising – you rarely think about anything *but* those exercises, so it really is a mindful practice that reduces pent-up emotions and can help to alleviate stress.

4. FILL UP ON JOY

Let's go back to my dream holiday of two weeks in Jamaica, with amazing food, sugary cocktails and full-body massages on the beach. That is the ultimate feeling of joy for me, but it's not something I can rely on all the time. There are simpler and more regular ways in which we can feel joy in our lives.

Joy, for me, is the smell of freshly baked bread; reading a good book while wrapped in a blanket; lighting some candles while watching a film; cuddling my partner; and, at the time of writing, feeling my baby boy in my womb. Think of something small that you can do to bring a smile instantly to your face.

5. CREATE A ROUTINE YOU CAN RELY ON

You need to build a routine around everything you do in your life, to help you with your mindfulness. Having a routine may seem boring but, over time, our bodies remember the little things we do and repeat every day, and they become habits. It gives us a sense of responsibility, and makes us accountable to ourselves too. Build a routine around your schedule so that you can be more efficient and effective, which will contribute to feeling more calm. Try these routines:

— A sleep routine: Aim to go to bed and wake up at the same time every day, so that your body can get into a rhythm and you can find your natural sleep cycle and wake-up clock.

— A morning routine: Wake up, make your bed, get washed and dressed (even if it's into loungewear), then rehydrate and refuel. Start the day with a small amount of productivity that will help you to go on to have a positive day.

> — An evening routine: Prepare your body for sleep by dimming the lights, closing your blinds and curtains, having a warm drink, getting into bed and reading.

You know the deal by now. These are just a few ideas, so take what you like and adapt them in a way that works for you.

HOLISTIC PRACTICES

I opened the book with my love for holistic and whole-istic health. It's something I am really passionate about, because the framework considers the whole person and not just a singular part of them. Holistic practices and healing modalities (the way in which something exists or is done; it also relates to the way someone experiences something) aim to bring a sense of relief, calm and alignment to mind, body and spirit. I love the idea of doing something that makes all of me feel better. Holistic healing is generally more expensive, because it tends to imply bespoke treatments. I find these more personable and interesting, and a sure way to process any stress in my body. A few of my favourites are:

I. REIKI

An alternative Japanese medicine that is used for energy healing and alignment, Reiki works with chakras (energy centres) and energy points within the physical body and the subtle emotional body to create flow and remove any congestion of emotions. The benefits of Reiki healing are that it reduces stress and anxiety, calms the emotions, increases blood flow and circulation, improves sleep – and so much more.

2. REFLEXOLOGY

This therapy works with pressure points in the feet, which are connected to other parts of our body, such as the liver and ovaries. By massaging and focusing on these pressure points, stress can be reduced and overall well-being can improve. The benefits of reflexology include the release of stagnant and suppressed emotions, a reduction in pain and a rebalancing of the body. On a personal level, reflexology changed my life, when I began to heal my body of childhood trauma. In the mornings I could barely walk on my feet, as they felt so sore and heavy, because I was holding on to so much pain. After weekly sessions over six months with my wonderful practitioner, Rashieda, I noticed a considerable difference in the way my feet felt. Some people find reflexology even more relaxing than a back massage.

3. EAR CANDLING

This is the practice of placing a lit cone in your ear, which, by means of the heat, enables wax to exit the ear. Ear candling can alleviate blocked sinuses and headaches. The lit cone can also contain certain essential oils, such as rosemary and geranium, that encourage relaxation.

4. CRANIOSACRAL THERAPY

This technique uses gentle touch on the skull and base of the neck to relieve blockages and trapped energy in the nervous system. It can also ease stress and tension that are being held in the skull and neck, which will eventually cause headaches.

5. AYURVEDA

Originating in India thousands and thousands of years ago, this modality is also known as 'the language of alignment'. Ayurveda uses food, massage, plants and much more to help people find balance and harmony in their mind, body and soul.

6. ACUPUNCTURE

This ancient Chinese technique uses incredibly thin, painless needles to unblock energy pathways in the body and relieve tension and stress.

As always, do your own research when it comes to different treatments and make sure that you seek out a trained professional.

PERSONAL PRACTICES

If you don't want, or can't afford, to hand over your wellness needs to someone else, there are things you can do to connect more with your body. They may be seen as everyday parts of your life, but you can find value and fun in them too. Engaging with your body in ways that you can control, and pouring your energy into activities you enjoy, will soothe and heal you.

I. MASTURBATING

If you're comfortable with exploring your body intimately, masturbation is a beneficial way to release a lot of feel-good hormones, as well as allowing your body to relax and let go of any pent-up tension. Masturbation can also be a good thing for you to do if you have experienced sexual trauma and wish to reclaim your body and your sexuality in a safe way, which you can control. Our sexual pleasure doesn't always have to result in an orgasm, and you can pleasure yourself without one and still feel amazing. This is an extremely personal choice; and if you don't feel comfortable about touching yourself intimately, explore the feelings you have around *why* masturbation is uncomfortable – what does it relate or connect too?

2. COOKING

I started to enjoy cooking in 2019. Due to past issues, cooking used to make me feel stressed, as I often made the meals I *thought* I should be cooking, instead of dishes I actually *wanted* to eat. I also hate following recipes and having to measure ingredients out precisely. To combat this, I bought a base set of ingredients whose flavour I liked and began cooking intuitively, adding my preferred seasonings and spices as I went. Even if I watch a recipe tutorial on YouTube, I still adapt it for myself – chucking in some all-purpose seasoning, onions and garlic for extra flavour! I find cooking a mindful act connected to nourishing my body and soul, and it makes me feel good that I am taking time out of my day to care for myself in this way.

Food can be a source of anxiety for so many people, due to the spread of 'diet culture' and society's incessant need to judge people by what they look like and what they *should* be eating. So it's imperative that we can reclaim and define our attitudes to food and develop a healthy approach to it. Regardless of the size or weight of our bodies, they need to be fuelled with nutrient-dense food, as well as eating the foods we enjoy. Where you can, give yourself enough time to prepare a good meal, and cook without judgement of yourself. And make it fun: put on some music when you cook, then enjoy the food by yourself or with others. From soul to bowl, baby, food is a form of love!

3. JOURNALING

If you follow me on social media, you will know how much I advocate journaling. I bang on about it all the time, because the positive impact it can have on people is amazing. Journaling is a way to connect to our subconscious, process emotions and release and rant about anything we need to. It's been a really helpful tool in my relationship, stopping me from calling my partner rude names to his face. Now I just journal it. It's also enabled me to recognise the things that are going on under the surface, and it's a handy log of all my emotions, helping me track how far I've come. I also love journaling because it's a place where I can be honest, raw and vulnerable, which is something we all struggle with. Journaling is a personal practice that enables us to hold space for ourselves. Build a routine around it: set the tone for your day, and create calm for your night. Try it!

THE POWER OF TALKING

When we talk about our feelings, we acknowledge them and give them the attention they deserve. If a feeling was pointless, it wouldn't be there in the first place. Our feelings demand to be felt and, if we don't do so, we suppress them, which can impact negatively on our well-being. I know it's a cliché, but relieving the burden of holding in our emotions can make us feel less alone and more connected to ourselves and others, as well as able to reflect on and process our feelings. Talking to others (especially people we know) about how we feel isn't always easy and may make us feel unsafe; in such instances I recommend speaking to the Samaritans or another mental-health charity that is trained in supporting you emotionally.

I also recommend speaking to yourself. When we put our feelings into words, we bring awareness to them and enable ourselves to be heard, which is so important. When we hear ourselves, we have the opportunity to evolve and grow emotionally. And feeling is a sign of self-respect.

THE POWER OF POSITIVE THINKING

We have around 6,000 thoughts per day, and most of them are fleeting and don't matter. Having the ability to think positively, remain aware of our thoughts and consciously choose not to get attached to our thinking is something we should all try to practise and fold into our daily lives. We barely give any attention to our mind, unless our negative thoughts are spiralling out of control. Then we panic, as we try to shut off our thoughts completely, but it's not that easy to pump the brakes and keep our mind quiet.

I really believe it's possible to think ourselves into a bad day. Think about it: you wake up, the weather is bleak outside, you go to the mirror and see a massive spot on your face. You then huff and puff and decide that today will be awful – so the day is awful. Nothing can shake you from that funk. You'll carry that same energy into everything you do that day. That's how powerful our thoughts are. On the flipside, if we can think ourselves into a bad day, we can also think ourselves into a good day.

I'm not saying that we should simply think positively all the time, because that would be a challenge and would cause us to live inauthentically, and what's positive about that? There's a term called 'toxic positivity': an excessive and ineffective use of being happy and optimistic in all situations. It can lead to avoidance, and to invalidation of our own very real feelings. For me, positive thinking means having a better awareness of our thoughts and practising 'intentional thinking' – knowing what we're thinking and being prepared to challenge or change the outcome. It's very possible that we can feel sadness and anger but also appreciation and gratitude at the same time.

I'm also a big believer that our thoughts become things; and that what we think in our internal world has the possibility to manifest in our external world, even if those external entities were not there to begin with. That is how powerful we are. We create our own realities by the thoughts we have, how strongly we believe in them and the perspectives we see through. I'm not going to act as if I'm a saint here. I have negative thoughts all the time; sometimes it's about my work, my body or the future. I complain when I feel uninspired, and I feel disappointment when I have setbacks. I'm only human, right? But when I hear those thoughts, I honour them and then replace them with positive ones. When I think I won't ever be able to buy my dream house, I change it to 'I will be able to buy a house when the time is right, and I'm financially able.' That's it. It really is that simple. Positive thinking isn't about not thinking negatively, because that would be too damn hard; it's just about not being too damn hard on yourself.

WELCOME, QUIET

If we are used to constant busyness and noise, welcoming in quietness and solitude can actually feel quite boring. Many of us have subconscious addictions to chaos, meaning that we are unaware of our need for drama to keep us satisfied, entertained and fulfilled. Being constantly 'on' and stimulated distracts us from difficult emotions, and ultimately stops us from doing any work on ourselves. When we press pause and slow down, we can begin to feel things we have suppressed, although this may be extremely uncomfortable - especially if we tend to keep ourselves busy as a way to push through life and get on with it. Welcoming in quiet benefits us in the long run, as it gives us time and space to acknowledge how we really feel, instead of pretending or putting on a mask. Welcoming in quiet also feels like rest, which we need so that our cells can renew and we are re-energised. Quiet time allows us to make sense of the world, alleviate any stressors and, of course, learn how to be alone.

AFFIRMATIONS

We can become more positive thinkers by paying attention to what we think and replacing negative thoughts with positive affirmations: simple yet powerful phrases and sentences that we can use to validate and assert who we are, who we want to be and where we are going. Saying affirmations daily enables them to penetrate our mindsets deeply, and although it is quite a simple practice, affirmations really do have a profound impact on us, even at a soul level. Repeating a certain phrase or sentence regularly over time becomes implanted inside us and remains within our core beliefs.

Affirmations are ways to reframe stories that we tell ourselves, and the perspectives and lenses we see those stories through. The most powerful phrases we can ever say start with 'I am', because essentially you are declaring to the universe what you believe about yourself and your reality. 'I can' is also a profound way to begin an intentional thought – and that is all affirmations are.

Here are a few of my go-to affirmations to combat my negative thoughts and retrain my brain to think positively. They follow the same word pattern: I am; I know; I trust; I believe; I accept; I love.

I AM:

I am enough as I am right now.	I am at home in my body.
I am powerful.	I am healing and I am healed.
I am divinely protected and guided.	I am healthy and whole today.
I am alive and living for today.	

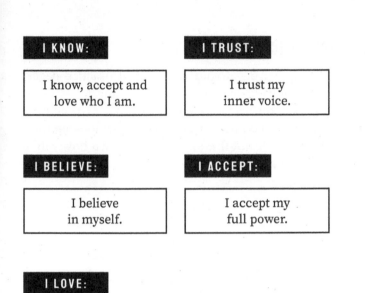

I KNOW:

I know, accept and
love who I am.

I TRUST:

I trust my
inner voice.

I BELIEVE:

I believe
in myself.

I ACCEPT:

I accept my
full power.

I LOVE:

I love and approve
of myself.

I love and appreciate
myself and others.

PRACTICE PAGES

You've arrived at your third set of practice pages. What holistic practices are you going to fold into your routine? What are your personal affirmations? Do you feel confident enough to start looking for a therapist? If not that's OK – write down how you're feeling here.

....

....

....

....

....

....

....

....

....

....

....

....

PRACTICE PAGES

....
....
....
....
....
....
....
....
....
....
....
....
....
....
....
....
....

PRACTICE PAGES

....
....
....
....
....
....
....
....
....
....
....
....
....
....
....
....
....

CHAPTER 4

CREATING BOUNDARIES

Creating boundaries is how we protect our peace, and they form the guidelines and rules that we put in place to communicate how we would like others to behave towards us. This includes access, manner of speech, needs and responsibilities between you and another person. Personal boundaries can be categorised as physical, sexual, emotional or social, and the extent of how important each boundary is to us will vary, depending on our preferences, our past experiences and our own individual values and comfort zones. While boundaries have a general scope, it's imperative to acknowledge that they can also be singular.

Learning boundaries begins with the limits that we place on ourselves and how we honour them. For us to be comfortable with our own boundaries, we have to stop self-betraying and self-abandoning by means of procrastination, not getting enough sleep, ignoring our feelings and working too much. When we neglect to meet our needs, we are allowing space for stress, illness, frustration and suffering. Our boundaries are there to protect us, but only if we use them properly. Boundaries can also be one of our greatest teachers, because they show us our limits and what we are, and are not, OK with, so that we have the capacity to really grow. Boundaries create and sustain healthy relationships, first with ourselves and then with others, and they need to be nurtured continually.

WHAT ARE YOUR LIMITS?

In order to set healthy boundaries, we have first to identify our needs – physical, emotional and social – and those times when we feel the boundaries that we create for ourselves are tested and overstepped. When our boundaries are not adhered to, we can feel resentment, anger, guilt and discomfort, some of which may be directed at ourselves, if we feel we are responsible. This is due to the fact that people sometimes overstep our boundaries because we unconsciously let them do so. We may have a need to be liked or needed, and this can manifest as being too available to others, which leaves us feeling drained, stressed and unappreciated.

Think about it: how many times have you taken on an extra shift at work when you didn't want to? How many times have you rescued a friend who missed their train or called in distress (when it wasn't that serious), because they knew you will always come running? These are just two examples of our boundaries being crossed, which depletes you and benefits others. Self-defining your boundaries is the process of determining what behaviour you will accept from others, and what you will not. And if we lack boundaries altogether, it is a sign that we are struggling with our sense of self and identity, and believe that we are unworthy of having healthy relationships. Try and be honest and direct with yourself, as this will help others: what is it you are prepared to do? And what are you *not* prepared to do?

PUTTING YOURSELF FIRST

Putting ourselves first will only seem selfish to those who gain something from our total lack of boundaries. Most of us will need to strengthen our boundaries in some way, due to the type of world in which we live. If we can give ourselves permission and time to strengthen our boundaries and honour the ways they will benefit our well-being, then we can begin to have agency over our lives, improve our confidence, make and maintain more healthy relationships and preserve our emotional energy.

LIMITING THOSE WHO ARE CLOSEST TO YOU

Enforcing boundaries within our own families is something many people struggle with. Boundaries don't always feel appropriate if you have been taught to put others before yourself, to ignore your own needs and suppress your emotions. But, as adults, we need to heal those wounds from the past and give ourselves permission to have limits within our relationships – regardless of whether those limits are with our own family.

We are supposed to learn boundaries as children, through our family dynamics and the responses and reactions that the adults in our lives have towards different situations and experiences. But for the most part, our parents and grandparents lacked healthy boundaries, because of generational trauma and a lack of ancestral healing. So here we are, in the twenty-first century, trying to learn what boundaries look like for us, and how to enforce them in order to protect our peace.

Boundaries within families can be super-hard, because sometimes parents have this weird notion that their children belong to them; at other times, toxic family members may perceive boundaries as a threat. But our home environment is where we should feel safe, secure and comfortable and, without any boundaries, our joy can be compromised and we may begin to feel angry, trapped and unhappy.

So having boundaries at home is a key component in protecting your own peace. Boundaries tell us, and others, what we believe is suitable behaviour; and what we will, and will not, accept. And *everyone* should have autonomy over themselves and their lives. Boundaries at home teach us the importance of boundaries in the outside world and how to act appropriately and responsibly – they are the bridge between 'This is how much I can love you' and 'This is how much I can love me – at the same time.'

Let's be honest here: friends and family members trigger reactions in us because they mirror back to us aspects of ourselves that we find difficult, or they walk paths that don't align with where we're heading. In moments like these, it's important to muster up the courage (if it is safe to do so) and have a conversation with them. In some instances that may not be the right thing to do, because of violence or other safety issues; and sometimes actually allowing a relationship to run its course and fizzle out is far more beneficial. Nonetheless, if it feels right, then a conversation is something that should be honoured.

And remember that it may feel right, but also extremely uncomfortable, which is quite normal (hello, intuition!). I have had to pull up my friends on their bullshit, and they have had to do the same to me – these are actually very healthy responses when a relationship needs to evolve. Just because something feels awkward and unpleasant doesn't mean it shouldn't happen. These moments are when growth happens. And isn't that what we are all striving for?

REACTING TO TRIGGERS

Triggers are simply things that need addressing and healing. In the moment they can feel all-consuming, but remember that they are not bigger or more powerful than you. If someone or something triggers you into a reaction, you can make a decision on how you want to move forward. Often our triggers are subconscious, but with self-awareness they start to become more and more obvious and, when they do, you can decide how to respond or react. You are stronger than you perceive, and if there is a niggling feeling that you need to speak up in order to choose yourself and release anxiety or stress, then do so! Bear in mind the following points:

— What people say and do is often a reflection of themselves and how they perceive the world and is rarely to do with you.

111

- Micro-aggressions stem from a place of bias, a lack of education and a lack of humanity and healing.

- Protecting your peace also means limiting your time with those your spirit rejects.

- If you're Black or a POC, it is not your responsibility to teach other people about race and privilege (*now read that again*).

- Your trauma is not your fault, but your healing is your responsibility.

DIGITAL DETOX

The access that other people have to you, and the ways in which you socialise and spend your time may be due in no small measure to social media. So try the following: limiting the time you spend on social media; revoking someone's access to you when they've been abusive; not allowing other people to trauma-dump; un-following people who make you feel bad about yourself; and leaving social situations when you've become bored or tired.

WORK–LIFE BALANCE

I'm not going to sugar-coat this: finding a balance between your working life and your personal life is bloody hard, and something I struggle with often. Some of us place so much of our self-worth on succeeding and achieving that slowing down and spending time doing other activities doesn't feel quite right. We are so conditioned to work, work, work that we often neglect our self-care, our relationships and our hobbies and enjoyment that sit outside making money or building a career. Other people may work too hard because that's all they know, and they have been encouraged to do so by parents or guardians; or they may be mirroring what other adults around them are doing. And then there are people who constantly work because they are avoiding feelings, people or situations they don't feel well equipped to handle. The reasons are endless, but the impact on our well-being is the same.

Our nervous systems go into overdrive when we don't spend time relaxing, having fun or socialising with the people we love. As humans, we literally crave intimacy and love, and how can those two emotions be nurtured if we are working all the time? Without a work–life balance, and adequate rest and time away from work, we end up feeling burnt out, stressed, fed up and angry. And while it's important we make money so that we can live and be able to afford hobbies and socialising, we also need to remember that it's vital to have boundaries when it comes to our working lives.

Your work–life balance has to be self-defined, because some people are perfectly happy and centred working more than fifty hours a week (I, for one, am definitely not) and other people would prefer to work thirty hours a week. However, I do believe that everyone should have enough time off that they feel well rested. Our nervous systems need to rest, so that our stress signals can rebalance, because without that break, our bodies cannot complete basic functions well. Our personal lives need nurturing and attention so that we feel fulfilment and joy, and that does not include the stimulation we may get in a working environment.

RELATIONSHIPS WITH OTHERS

It is in our human nature to engage in relationships, both platonic and romantic, and to develop healthy attachments and a healthy dependency on others. I, for one, have learnt so much about myself through friendships and past relationships – even if they didn't last too long. We can gain so much knowledge and self-awareness from others through our own projections and what they mirror back to us. So being able to manage and maintain relationships is crucial for our well-being, and particularly the social, emotional and intellectual dimensions of our lives. Relationships sit on a whole spectrum of intimacy, vulnerability, connection, support, trust, honesty and acceptance. And often what we get and give in one relationship will differ from the next one – and being an emotionally developed adult will really teach you this.

RESPECTING OTHERS

The other dynamic of boundaries is how *we* react and respond to *other* people. We've learnt by now that relationships are an absolute essential in a whole and fulfilled life, and a part of that need is being able to respect other people, especially when it comes to *their* boundaries. We know that boundaries are essential for our own well-being and happiness, and therefore we need to recognise the importance of them for other people. It can be easy to constantly put on the 'victim' hat and blame other people for our relationships breaking down, but sometimes the issue really isn't them. Finding someone else's boundaries difficult is not their problem, it is yours; and you will need to explore your own feelings and take responsibility for them.

When we overstep another person's boundaries, we are essentially saying, 'I don't respect you or acknowledge the parameters of your peace', which is a pretty shitty thing to do. I understand that we may subconsciously do this for reasons relating to our past or previous traumas, but as adults we cannot use these as excuses – we need to move forward and have authority over the decisions we make. When we become more self-aware, our subconscious thoughts, feelings and actions will then become conscious – making processes like this much easier.

PRACTICE PAGES

You've arrived at your fourth set of practice pages. What steps are you going to take to create effective boundaries? How will you put space between your work and life? Are there any relationships that you want to change or improve?

....
....
....
....
....
....
....
....
....
....
....
....

PRACTICE PAGES

....
....
....
....
....
....
....
....
....
....
....
....
....
....
....
....

CHAPTER 5

LeTTiNG GO

There is an African proverb I often turn to that says, 'When you let go of what others think about you, how something is going to turn out, or how your past will affect your future, then you are finally living a free life.' Have you ever found yourself holding on to people, situations and old parts of who you once were? Maybe you're not even aware of it, but for lots of different reasons we remain in the past and fixated on certain aspects that, more often than not, make us miserable. Living in the past is not the same as going back to your past to process your trauma and emotions. One is conscious and intentional; the other is not.

Trauma (which I'll talk about more in the next chapter) often prevents us from letting go. It keeps us rooted in our past, reliving and replaying memories over and over again. Our memories are not just confined to our minds; memories can be more physical and can show up in our bodies too. Memories can be what we eat, what we smell and what we hear. At times such memories can trigger us to have a physical reaction in the present moment, or can make us dissociate and disconnect from ourselves, so that we don't need to feel any difficult emotions. Quite often, when we are replaying an experience that happened to us, we are seeing life through the eyes of a much younger version of ourselves – someone different from the person we are today. Experiencing this point of view over and over again creates a constant cycle of stress, suffering and anxiety.

Another aspect that prevents us from letting go is the amount of blame we place on ourselves. We may feel as if the cause of something was our fault, so we experience an immense sense of shame and guilt, which immobilises us even further, preventing us from moving on. In order to begin letting go, we need to talk about our experiences, honour our feelings and the person we used to be and acknowledge how much we have grown. We have to step into the person we are now – and the person we hope to be. Only then can we begin to let go of the little storm trapped within us.

LETTING GO OF ANXIETY

The scary and yet empowering thing about life is that much of it lies beyond our control. Yes, we have a schedule to follow – whether it is getting up to go to work, having your lunch at the same hour every day, going to your weekly workout class or going on that yearly holiday. We make plans that we try to keep. We have routines, which keep us

121

stable. We set out goals and intentions to achieve. However, sometimes events happen unexpectedly; there's no planning or accounting for it – it just happens. Your morning bus could be late, the boiler could break down, your class or your holiday could be cancelled. If we don't have the right tools to let go in that moment, we can create anxiety within ourselves that follows us.

Anxiety consists of small amounts of stress that build up over time, causing excessive feelings of fear, apprehension and anticipation. And while anxiety is a very normal and natural response to feeling stressed out, the amount of anxiety that people feel is not. Low levels of anxiety can be uncomfortable at worst, but they're usually fleeting and don't tend to last very long. However, people who experience chronic anxiety typically feel anxious on a daily basis, and this will routinely affect their lives in lots of different ways.

Letting go can be difficult because it asks us to pay attention to what is going on inside us, and encourages us to have faith and hope in the unknown. We need to be aware that there are some aspects we simply can't control. We often feel resistance to letting go because we're afraid of 'going with the flow'. The ancient Chinese philosopher Chuang Tzu once said,

'Flow with whatever is happening and let your mind be free. Stay centred by accepting whatever you are doing.' Going with the flow means letting go of control. It means taking away your reason for anxiety by declaring there is nothing you can do about it. It's throwing caution to the wind, and saying: 'Be free and be calm.'

Another source of resistance to going with the flow is because we want to portray ourselves as having our shit together. We care far too much about the perceptions of others, and lack self-compassion towards the wild and messy parts of ourselves. One thing I've learnt on my ever-evolving journey of self is that where there is mess, there is life. Around us there are millions of atoms leaping, unknown and known planets orbiting – the entirety of creation in itself is a mess. Why, then, should we be any different?

PROCESSING YOUR PAST

To begin to let go, we must deal with our past and, until we process it, it will often feel like it's here right now and is still affecting us. The past consciously and unconsciously affects where we are in the moment. We all operate from past experiences, stories and scripts that we tell ourselves, as well as according to beliefs and morals that we have been told and shown through family, guardians and people who have had an impact upon us. Until we become aware of how much this has programmed us and conditioned our habits, and of the inner voices that we may hear, we will struggle to live in the present moment.

We can't erase what we've been through or the memories we have, but eventually we can make peace with the past and let it go. If we continue to hold on, we remain stuck and therefore struggle to enjoy the life we have right now. We process the past by giving ourselves space and time to feel; by expressing our emotions and holding no attachment to, or judgement of, them; by releasing our emotions, forgiving others as well as ourselves and allowing ourselves to grieve; and by making new memories and showing gratitude for who we were, and who we are right now.

EXPRESSING YOUR EMOTIONS

Stop suppressing your emotions, and express them instead. Emotions left sitting inside you will not only affect you emotionally, but physically too. Those pent-up feelings will reside in your body, causing aches, pains and ailments. Talking about our feelings is imperative to overall health, and also teaches us the importance of communication with our loved ones and our communities. However, if this doesn't seem like a viable option for you, communicate with yourself by sending yourself a voice-note, or picking up pen and paper and just writing it down. I talk about journaling a lot because it is such a cathartic process. It can be good to have a record of what was holding you back, so that you can see how far you've come.

RELEASING YOUR EMOTIONS

Releasing your emotions doesn't mean constantly crying or screaming into your pillow, although both of these may be extremely beneficial and are something I do quite often, but we can release our pent-up feelings through exercise. Exercise is a wonderful way to engage with your body, connect to it and let go. Exercise is not just about changing your body weight or size, it's a vital part of caring for your body. It is a way to clear your mind and create space inside you by removing any emotional and physical blockages.

Exercise doesn't need to be boring or painful, and can be light-hearted and fun, but it's up to us to change that narrative for ourselves. Exercise is for *everybody*, regardless of what they look like, and it's important that we all remember this. Exercise is something we need to reclaim and redefine for ourselves, especially for plus-size bodies, less-abled bodies and anyone who doesn't have the 'ideal' body type. I've mentioned these techniques before, but simple meditation is a gateway to our innate power, and conscious breathwork is engaging enough to shift suppressed emotions. Outside validation is available for everything – we simply need to breathe; the power lies with us.

GIVING YOURSELF SPACE AND TIME

Letting go is about your personal surroundings and your environment too! When energy disperses or emotions are released, they remain in the air around you until they are cleared, so it's important to cleanse our spaces. Have you ever walked into a room and its energy hit you? Or have you entered your space after being out all day and the room felt so cluttered and engulfing? These are signs that you might need to do a cleanse. You can do this by decluttering, recycling and organising, but you can also do it by smudging.

Smudging is a sacred ceremony practised by indigenous Americans, whereby sacred herbs (and sometimes medicines) are burnt for cleansing or ritual purposes and for inviting in good energy. Smudging can also be used for bodily health and for healing. The safest and most environmentally friendly way to smudge your chosen space is by using incense. Sage and Palo Santo are most commonly used, but they are at risk of being over-harvested, which in turn impacts on the lives and well-being of indigenous people. Incense is more readily available and comes in a wide range of scents to suit different moods and needs. I prefer to be proactive with cleansing rituals rather than reactive, which is why I burn incense daily, clearing my space without even thinking about it. If you're not fond of incense, or it will interfere with an existing health condition, make sure you open the windows in your home or space regularly – preferably every morning and every night (crack them open a little in winter) – to release stagnant and stale energy.

FORGIVING YOURSELF AND OTHERS

It's hard to let go when we are holding on to the pain and turmoil caused by someone else in our lives, and it will get even harder if we don't recognise the role we had to play in that story. We aren't perfect human beings, and sometimes our decisions and choices have a negative impact on others as well as on ourselves. We cannot move forward until we practise forgiveness. The negative assumptions around forgiveness are that it makes you weak, you've admitted defeat or are accepting the pain caused to you. Actually, forgiveness simply means that all the emotions you have about what occurred, or about a particular person, no longer serve you. Holding on – when we need to let go – stops our progress and happiness, so we actively need to make a choice to liberate ourselves. If something no longer has meaning or purpose for us, then it is simply a burden and we must lighten the load. Even if you are unable to forgive others just yet, forgiving yourself should be high on your priority list. Self-forgiveness is a step towards self-discovery, because when you forgive yourself, you are accepting who you are right now. Let go of what happened, what you did and who you were.

GRIEF

The process of grief is so important because without it, we cannot let go and move forward. How can we possibly move on with our lives if we have yet to unravel and face the grief of losing parts of ourselves? Grief that hasn't been acknowledged keeps us in the past and rooted in who we were back then. For some people this can mean that they are adults in the present, but operating from their teenage or even child selves. Grief isn't simply about someone passing away; it can be about not receiving a safe and secure childhood, or experiencing some kind of trauma that alters the trajectory of your life. This can actually feel like a death, and that is so valid. Parts of us have survived and other parts of us have died, and we have to accept that, in order to begin to rebuild our lives and focus on who we are now. Grieving is a natural response to loss (of any kind) and really can be exhausting, but once we get through it – or at least learn to live with the loss – then the heaviness begins to lift, giving us more energy as we move forward.

MAKING NEW MEMORIES

Failing to let go can root us in the past too much, making us neglectful of the moments and the people we surround ourselves with now. Making new memories could involve anything – for me, it's built on socialising, inviting a sense of enjoyment into my life. Do something that makes you smile, long after it's happened, whether that's going to a funfair, eating out with friends or staying out late; bonding with your friends over a movie that's bound to make you cry; going to a concert; laughing until you wee; making love with the person of your dreams; doing karaoke, even though you can't sing; sleeping in until midday and watching your favourite old movies; trying a new food; telling a random stranger that you like their outfit. The examples are endless!

SHOWING GRATITUDE FOR WHO YOU ARE

There are some basic rituals and practices that not only make us feel better, but shift and reshape our energy so that our vibrations have a higher frequency. Showing gratitude is a simple practice to enable us to reconnect to our lineage, our ancestral plains and the generations that came before us. Gratitude welcomes in more positive feelings and attitudes, which can help us change our perspectives and see some good in ourselves and in the world. Being grateful for what you have sends positive energy out into the world, encouraging and manifesting even more positive things to come your way. To show gratitude is to be connected to the Divine.

PRACTICE PAGES

You've arrived at your fifth set of practice pages. What steps do you need to work on to help you let go? What are some new memories you want to create moving forward?

....
....
....
....
....
....
....
....
....
....
....
....
....

PRACTICE PAGES

....
....
....
....
....
....
....
....
....
....
....
....
....
....
....
....
....

CHAPTER 6

DEALING WITH TRAUMA

So much of our pain, confusion and lack of emotional stability stems from our trauma wounds, which can go unresolved and remain unhealed for quite a period of time. A traumatic event can be defined as an incident that causes someone harm on a physical, emotional, spiritual or psychological level. The person in distress may feel anxious and frightened, but in some cases an emotion may not register at all. Trauma can come from anywhere. You might experience a fatal traffic accident or undergo serious medical surgery. You may have been the victim of sexual abuse, assault or childhood neglect, or may have experienced the death of a friend or relative. Whatever your personal experience, it will impact upon your mental health and nervous system with a complete overload of stress. This can manifest itself, either outwardly or inwardly on your body, in the form of anxiety, eating disorders, physical illness, difficulty in sleeping, reduced concentration or an overwhelming sense of shame and sadness – to name but a few.

IDENTIFYING YOUR TRIGGERS

Triggers are a reminder of a past traumatic experience, an occurrence that prompts the remembering of the disturbing event. The trigger itself is not always frightening. A trigger can be a scent, a noise, a look, a word said in passing by someone, or one that you can't say yourself. To feel triggered is to experience severe emotional distress that may result in dissociation, avoidance behaviours or fatal actions where you injure yourself. Your triggers can be internal too, such as feeling an intense sense of loneliness and abandonment. It's important to identify your own triggers, and a good way to start is by being aware of what's going on around you when you feel 'triggered'. An integral part is taking time out to feel the sensations within your body, so that you are then able to catch them before you erupt or get distressed.

Question every emotion that you experience when you feel triggered, every thought racing through your head and how your body feels. Take to that trusted pen-and-paper method that I love so much – journaling, or write your thoughts in the Notes section of your phone. It's important to record your feelings for your own benefit, and if you are seeking professional help to get you through and process your trauma. If it's safe for you to do so, and it won't impact on someone else's mental health and well-being, talk to someone close to you.

Triggers are the subconscious areas of us that are asking to be seen, processed and healed. We can't always eradicate them, because sometimes they are part of normal day-to-day life, but what we can do is become aware of how we respond to them, so that we can manage ourselves in a more appropriate way. The word 'triggered' has been co-opted by popular culture, used as a term in moments of banter when someone feels uncomfortable or seen. I believe that overuse of this word is having a detrimental impact on mental-health awareness and on the word's legitimate meaning. It takes away the impact that a trigger can have, and the honesty it can bring someone, and we shouldn't make light of how important that is.

GENERATIONAL TRAUMA

Generational or transgenerational trauma is a type of trauma that can be passed from the first generation of survivors to their children, and to further generations over time. It sits within our spiritual DNA, and will continue to be passed down our lineage unless healing occurs. In recent years the focus on generational trauma has been explored within the Black diaspora – the generational trauma from enslavement still follows us.

Generational trauma can often become normalised as 'That's just the way our family does things', because of how ingrained it has become within the family system, without unpicking how it came about, or the effects it could have if we let it continue. Breaking the chain of ancestral trauma can be extremely difficult, especially as Black people are still oppressed and experiencing the effects of the legacy of enslavement, which led to systemic racism, 'misogynoir' – the prejudice against Black women – and the continuance of white supremacy. Generational trauma can also show up in addictive tendencies such as drug abuse, but also in poverty and mental illness.

A lot of the time our parents and guardians are operating from a place of trauma. This can result in dysfunctional child–parent relationships, harmful patterns of behaviour and beliefs, and the normalisation of unhealthy behaviours and boundaries between family members. It can be very traumatic to broach the past with our families, so you need to recognise that it may take time; and you, as the instigator, must be ready and determined to break the cycle. Becoming more aware of our family history will enable us to feel more compassion for ourselves and family members, both past and present. It will also give us a greater understanding of why we are the way we are; and it will contribute to ending a cycle of abuse or pain ingrained in our lineage, which will heal us and free us.

There are a few different ways in which you can connect with your ancestors – both living and dead – in order to embrace this process:

1. Speak to them, if they are willing. Remember them, if they are gone.

2. Visualise them during your meditations.

3. Book a session with an ancestral healer.

4. Research your family tree as far back as you can go, and record it.

5. Light some candles for your ancestors, and invite them to give you a sign.

PERSONAL TRAUMA

Personal trauma, unlike generational trauma, relates to our own individual experiences and the way they have made us feel. One person may experience exactly the same traumatic event as you, but will perceive it differently – so it's important that we show compassion and empathy towards the way we feel. Personal trauma, especially childhood trauma, is not your fault, but processing it and working through it is your responsibility – annoying as that may often be. I'll be the first to admit that trauma can definitely create resentment towards the other people involved, particularly if we were children who were traumatised by adults.

Personal trauma may have been part of your life for what feels like forever, but it doesn't always have to be that way – and it won't, if you work towards change. Regulating your emotions, finding purpose and meaning, talking through your feelings and having someone listen to them, and taking care of yourself through multi-dimensional well-being gives you the best chance of healing and becoming emotionally well.

PRACTICE PAGES

You've arrived at your sixth set of practice pages. This chapter wasn't easy. What do you need to pack into your self-care toolbox to help you deal with your trauma?

....

....

....

....

....

....

....

....

....

....

....

....

....

PRACTICE PAGES

....

....

....

....

....

....

....

....

....

....

....

....

....

....

....

....

PRACTICE PAGES

....
....
....
....
....
....
....
....
....
....
....
....
....
....
....
....
....

CHAPTER 7

YOU HAVE IT IN YOU TO HEAL

I wish I could give you all the answers on how to calm your mind, and tell you that self-care can completely change your life, but that isn't always the case. Self-care can, however, make our lives more relaxed and less stressful; it can create self-awareness and self-compassion, and it can help us to slow down and find balance. But while this may be enough for some people, unfortunately it won't be enough for others. We also need resources and access to professional support – for everyone and anyone, regardless of class, race or gender – because people are suffering from immense distress and other issues relating to trauma.

If you're reading this and nodding your head, then I feel for you, I hear you and I see you. It often feels as if we are banging our heads against the wall, asking the government for funding and money to help a society that is suffering mentally and physically. I often feel like shouting – 'hello, can anyone hear me'. Mental Health Awareness Weeks simply aren't enough anymore, and conversations need to evolve beyond speaking up and speaking out, because what happens after we do that? Where are the support and the services? I don't want to be a complete Negative Nancy, but I think it's important to highlight that a lack of resources and access to mental-health support are real problems in Britain, and we cannot continue pretending they're not.

Nonetheless, I don't want you to feel bummed out or stuck, or as if you can't possibly do anything to make yourself feel that little bit better, because you can. And I hope that with this book and your own mental-health toolbox, you *believe* that you have it in you, because you do. You are capable, you are strong and you are able to get to know yourself at a profound level, and then unlearn and relearn whatever you need to. Recognising where you're unbalanced and taking small, simple steps will be extremely beneficial to you over time, especially in a world that feels highly stimulating and overwhelming. We do not need to live the way capitalism tells us we have to; and we sure as hell do not need to walk through life pretending we're OK when we're not.

You are worthy and deserving of being mindful in your choices and your decisions, so that you can look back when you're eighty and think, 'Fuck, I really lived the life I wanted to, and not a life that was given to me.' Of course seeking outside help, in the form of a counsellor or therapist, a spiritual healer or life coach, can help massively towards finding a greater sense of connection and peace, but ultimately a professional stands with you and holds your hand while you go on this journey of self-exploration. Regardless, you have it in you to calm your thoughts and heal your body. Nobody else can sort out your shit except you, and I implore you always to remember that. Healing takes time, and time is a healer. You have got this!

Now let's take a look at your mental-health toolbox.

CREATING A WELL-BEING TOOLBOX

Your well-being toolbox should be full of all the things that make you feel less stressed, calmer and a little bit more you. Within this toolbox you should have affirmations, mindful techniques and a list of ways in which you can process your feelings, relax and switch off. This toolbox needs to be individual and self-defined, so that you can lean on it, come rain or shine. Developing it may feel a little odd at first but, over time, your mental-health toolbox will become familiar and you will start to see the benefits of it.

When we have a well-being toolbox, it gives us a gentle reminder of ways to come home to ourselves, which we often need when we're stressed, distressed or feeling lost. In your toolbox you should have a list of all the techniques that enable you to feel calm, connected and centred. It might be stroking your arm as a way to self-soothe, going for a walk to calm your anxiety or talking to friends to help with feelings of loneliness. Your toolbox is an action plan – a way to take control of your own well-being and do as much as you can to feel balanced and in alignment.

Your toolbox can even be a physical box, if that's more your thing, and you can fill it with written affirmations, favourite photos, candles, incense and essential oils. Again, make sure it is self-defined and relatable to *you* and whatever makes *you* feel better. If you need a starting point, here are some mindful techniques for your well-being toolbox.

1. Journal your thoughts and feelings.

2. Go for a walk, even if it's raining, because rain is a clearing energy.

3. Talk to someone close to you or a trained professional.

4. Put on some music and allow yourself to *feel*.

5. Go for a massage.

6. Get in touch with a charity or the NHS for mental health support.

7. If prescribed, take your medications.

8. Fill up your hot-water bottle, get under a blanket and watch your favourite film.

9. Release emotions through crying or screaming.

10. Stretch your limbs and connect to your body.

11. Do breath work until you feel calmer.

12. Do something that makes you laugh.

13. Clean and declutter the space around you.

14. Donate your time to someone else.

15. Read positive affirmations.

16. Do a guided meditation.

17. Water your plants, if you have them.

18. Make something to eat and drink some water.

19. Read a book.

20. Take a long, hot bath

YOUR MENTAL HEALTH TOOLBOX

....

....

....

....

....

....

....

....

....

....

....

....

....

....

....

....

YOUR MENTAL HEALTH TOOLBOX

....

....

....

....

....

....

....

....

....

....

....

....

....

....

....

....

....

....

CONCLUSiON

Wow, we've reached the end of *How To Calm It*. By this point I hope you feel more aware and empowered to do whatever you need to do to live a less stressful life.

When we have a poor work–life balance, subconscious trauma responses, a lack of understanding of who we are and insufficient access to professional mental-health support, our nervous systems are in complete overdrive. We work too hard, suppress our emotions and put other people before ourselves, resulting in a disconnected and unbalanced life, which simply cannot be sustained in a healthy way. To feel calm we need to acknowledge how we operate and why, how we feel and what works for us, in terms of managing our thoughts and our emotions.

We are all extremely different, and it's vital that we understand the importance of choosing who we would like to be, instead of allowing our conditioning and programming to choose for us. *We* are the ones in control of our lives. Throughout society, stress is normalised, thus creating a world full of anxiety, lack of self-care and very poor boundaries, but it does not have to be this way. I hope this book serves as a reminder that *you* matter, that you're important and that your health should come first. Through multi-dimensional well-being, your wellness toolbox, self-compassion and empathy – as well as self-exploration of your culture, your childhood experiences and mindful practices – you can really begin to live a life that is for *you*.

everyday Resources

Here are some books, Instagram accounts and hashtags that I recommend you welcome into your life. These will challenge you, make you think, inspire you, educate you, boost your confidence and your ability to create a more connected and expansive life.

What we digest has an impact on our well-being, so it's important that you take in meaningful, positive and awakening content to help you with your personal development. Social media, as we all know, can be pretty damaging, if we aren't mindful of who we are following and what we read. Take this as a sign to create an online space that makes you feel good!

PEOPLE TO FOLLOW ON INSTAGRAM

@bodyimage_therapist
@nedratawwab
@scarrednotscared
@silvykhoucasian
@the.holistic.psychologist

@thenutritiontea
@wetheurban
@blackmindsmatter.uk
@howtohealholistically
@emma.the.alchemist
@softpathhealing
@blackgirlom
@iamrachelricketts
@iambrillyant
@yung_peublo
@thy.self

#consciousness
#healing
#innerchild
#spiritualgrowth
#soulpurpose

BOOKS TO READ

Akala, *Natives: Race and Class in the Ruins of Empire* (Two Roads, 2019)

Maya Angelou, *And Still I Rise* (Virago Press, 1986)

Linda Bacon, *Health at Every Size* (BenBella Books, 2010)

Jasmin Lee Cori, *Healing from Trauma: A Survivor's Guide* (Da Capo Press, 2008)

Amir Levine & Rachel Heller, *Attached: Are You Anxious, Avoidant or Secure?* (Bluebird, 2019)

Donna Jackson Nakazawa, *Childhood Disrupted* (Atria Books, 2015)

Lucy H. Pearce, *Moon Time* (Womancraft Publishing, 2015)

David Richo, *How to Be an Adult in Relationships* (Shambhala Publications, 2002)

Geneen Roth, *Women Food and God* (Simon & Schuster, 2011); might be triggering for those with eating issues

Neale Donald Walsch, *Conversations with God* (Hodder and Stoughton, 2019)

Marianne Williamson, *A Return to Love* (Harper Thorsons, 2015)

PROFESSIONAL SUPPORT

www.blackmindsmatteruk.com
www.baatn.org.uk
www.counselling-directory.org.uk
www.mind.org.uk
www.studentminds.org.uk

ACKNOWLEDGEMENTS

A massive thank you to the #Merky Books team for such an exciting opportunity, and for approaching me with a project I could get my teeth stuck into. I'm grateful that I am *finally* able to write about things that really matter to me.

An even bigger thank you to Megan Staunton from Gleam Titles, who has been with me through the months of writing this book and has supported me – even with my raging pregnancy hormones.

To my manager, Milly Mils, who I love dearly, and who has held my hand every step of the way – sometimes even having to drag my feet too, lol – *you are an angel* and 'thank you' doesn't even cut it.

And lastly to my partner, Lee, for being my biggest cheerleader; to my followers who have watched me grow; and to *you*, the reader, for buying this book and allowing my words to reflect the light that is already inside you. Oh, and to the universe, to Source, to God: thank you for blessing me with the essence of life. *Big up youuuuuuuu allll!*

Grace Victory is an award-winning digital-first creator, predominately known for her inspiring words, powerful vulnerability and refusal to diminish her self, values or voice, to suit societal expectations. Through her passion for female advocacy, unflinching honesty and encouraging spirit, Grace talks openly about topics that are perceived taboo; therapy, sex, trauma, relationship dynamics, diet culture, self-awareness and spirituality. Grace's content focuses on healing the mind, body and spirit and the importance of self-development, alongside sharing her personal journey.

Black Minds Matter UK is a charity and initiative on a mission to create a safe space for Black people to be offered mental health support by Black therapists in the UK. Created by Agnes Mwakatuma and Annie Nash in June 2020, Black Minds Matter has three clear goals: to connect Black people with certified Black therapists, to improve mental health resources for the Black community through the NHS, and to tackle the stigma surrounding mental health in and outside of the Black community.

NOTES

NOTES

NOTES

NOTES

UNLOCK YOUR POTENTIAL WITH THE *HOW TO* SERIES

AVAILABLE NOW